Radiant Voices

RADIANT VOICES

21 Feminist Essays for Rising Up

Inspired by EMMA Talks

Edited by carla bergman

BRINDLE
AND GLASS

Brindle & Glass
An imprint of TouchWood Editions
Touchwoodeditions.com

The information in this book is true and complete to the best of the authors' knowledge. All recommendations are made without guarantee on the part of the authors or the publisher.

Editing and arrangement by carla bergman
Art on front cover and inside covers by Julie Flett
Cover design by Tree Abraham
Interior design by Colin Parks

LIBRARY AND ARCHIVES CANADA CATALOGUING IN PUBLICATION

Title: Radiant voices : 21 feminist essays for rising up inspired by EMMA Talks / edited by carla bergman.

Names: bergman, carla, editor.

Identifiers: Canadiana 20190148322 | ISBN 9781927366844 (softcover)

Subjects: LCSH: Feminism.

Classification: LCC HQ1155 .R33 2019 | DDC 305.42—dc23

TouchWood Editions gratefully acknowledges that the land on which we live and work is within the traditional territories of the Lkwungen (Esquimalt and Songhees), Malahat, Pacheedaht, Scia'new, T'Sou-ke and W̱SÁNEĆ (Pauquachin, Tsartlip, Tsawout, Tseycum) peoples.

We acknowledge the financial support of the Government of Canada through the Canada Book Fund and the Canada Council for the Arts, and of the Province of British Columbia through the British Columbia Arts Council and the Book Publishing Tax Credit.

The interior pages of this book have been printed on 100% post-consumer recycled paper, processed chlorine free, and printed with vegetable-based inks.

Printed in Canada at Houghton Boston

19 20 21 22 23   5 4 3 2 1

For LJB, the radiant one

Once upon a time, when
women were birds, there was
the simple understanding
that to sing at dawn and to
sing at dusk was to heal the
world through joy. The birds
still remember what we have
forgotten, that the world
is meant to be celebrated.
– Terry Tempest Williams

Contents

Hovering

Roses offer their scent
it travels through my
body
remembering
when I could fly.
Vibrations responding
    aroma whispering

the shivers up and down your spine
are because your wings are becoming

— carla bergman

There's really no such thing as the 'voiceless'. There are only the deliberately silenced or the preferably unheard.

– Arundhati Roy

Introduction

carla bergman

Let us take a moment to celebrate the eruption of radiant voices. Because previously unheard voices and stories are being shared en masse—more and more folks from the margins are making their stories public, and more importantly, these voices are being listened to and amplified. From Idle No More to #BlackLivesMatter to #MeToo, one thing is certain: landscapes are shifting. These beautiful eruptions are happening rapidly like never before—in part because of the internet and social media's speed and accessibility, but also because years of hard, subtle work by individuals and collective organizers whose work has enabled deep, below-the-ground listening, and being there for each other. Acts of care in intimate community relationships empower people to share in public for the first time. These messages from below are where my hope for a better future comes from—new and old stories being shared, new possibilities being unearthed.

Shifts that take hold and provide real change take time. We are up against centuries of structural violence and oppression justified by narratives of dominance that shift to survive. Often these narratives remain the loudest, amplified and shared not only by media and institutions but in our homes. Yet, there is hope—because there are cracks everywhere in the dominant order, and these powers are fragile, especially when we work together.

We can combat these devastating patriarchal holds on our lives by collectively committing more to listening to non-dominant voices, especially in subtle, curious, generative ways, and to also listen out loud—all of us, everywhere, saying loudly, "I hear you. I believe you. I want to know more!" An upwelling of sharing and being heard can shift things in ways we cannot fully predict or imagine, and there are countless ways for it to happen: speech, writing, other forms of expressions and actions, art, and new and loving ways of being in relationships that cut across difference. But ultimately, we need listeners, readers, and viewers; we need dialogue, and we need all of us.

This work must happen in all areas of public and private life. Countless folks are creating spaces and platforms, yet many still face barriers—especially young, Black, disabled, Indigenous, gender-non-conforming, and other marginalized folks. Moving into public life can be terrifying, even unsafe, so we need a collective push, especially from those of us with privilege and social capital: we all need to commit to amplifying and nurturing those who are not always heard. We must co-create inclusive, nurturing platforms by being open and flexible, and spaces that offer them safety. We need to profoundly trust that they know what they need to say. We must commit to listening with care and be open to the creation of rapid change. This is feminist listening.

Threads running through my collaborative work over the past dozen years include radical social change, amplification of voices at the edges, and a connection between emerging voices and seasoned folks. Projects have ranged in scope and platform from print to live talks. *Radiant Voices* is the offshoot of one such project, EMMA Talks, a feminist speaker series and mini–art festival held in Vancouver, BC. (See pages 5–9.)

I have been deeply interested in social access, ways to listen and hold space for one another, and ongoing conversation about needed change. My work emphasizes the invitation and inclusion of rarely heard voices alongside well-known folks, which to me is necessary for profound mutual aid. Though not always straightforward, this curation style runs through my artistic and community engagement. At the centre of this style is my desire to celebrate stories of thriving—the everyday breakthroughs and successes we achieve individually, collectively, and politically. My goal is to inspire, evoke change, and provide courage that enables us to act in solidarity and engage more passionately with our own powers.

In my early work, I tended to work with children and youth. Over time, my work has come to include a multitude of projects and voices. Many of these changes emerged through incredible collaboration in which we, the many youth, friends and fellow artists, heard one another, tuned into shifts in our and others' lives, and from that determined what we needed to thrive and have joy. This past has now brought me to *Radiant Voices*, whose brilliant and creative contributors have made this project a complete joy to create.

ABOUT THIS BOOK

The idea for this book came from the wonderful publisher Taryn Boyd, who thought to create a companion book of the talks from EMMA to date. I immediately loved the idea but added a bit of a twist—*Radiant Voices* includes some talks from EMMA as well as new material by writers and artists not from EMMA: essays, a visual narrative, and poems. I saw this book as another platform and wanted to invite folks who, for a variety of reasons, might be unable to give talks in public. I also wanted to incorporate other ways of sharing stories.

Like EMMA Talks, I did not instruct folks on what to say in their essays. For this reason, the book has several themes and a diversity of writing styles and voices. This is intentional: a handful of the essays are from public talks, so they feature a variety of communication styles and a curated multiplicity of perspectives. Some of the EMMA Talks speakers' pieces are personal narratives; others are essays about ideas and histories; still others are a mix of both. Key themes guiding my curation came from the essays and poems themselves: finding voice; our personal, collective, and political power; love; celebration; matriarchy; connection; and belonging. What emerged is a feminist anthology of unique, diverse, personal, and fiercely political stories. And because our stories and ideas need to be heard and felt in other ways, too, I have also included poetry and visuals. My poem "Taking Flight" sews the book together. Its stanzas each begin one of the book's five sections, including the introduction. The poem was inspired not only by the essays in this collection, but by Julie Flett's art, which appears on the front cover, and inside front and back covers of this book. These three images tell a visual story she calls "kitotitowak." The image on the inside front cover represents, to me, a finding of each other's voice, the inside back cover represents a coming together to share, with the front cover exemplifying flight and soaring.

I am thrilled with these themes; I believe reading others' stories of love and belonging can connect us and help us feel less alone. Connection is at the heart of our survival and our thriving. When we feel connected, seen, and heard—when we truly feel our belonging—we feel more alive, capable, and loved. Even in our darkest times, love persists. Feeling our connection is vital to (re)imagining how we can be otherwise, especially in these troubled times. We need to hear stories and new ideations that inspire us to, together, fight, love, and take back our power. Let us continue listening to more folks' stories of struggle, love, discovery, joy, and belonging.

For far too long, the stories we have heard, even within radical movements, have primarily been told by white cis men, who simply do not represent the many important voices of individuals throughout the spectrum of genders, sexual orientation, and backgrounds. That is not to say that white, cis men do not have a voice—they do—but it's important to acknowledge that the stories they have shared often do not represent everyone. We know there is a deep undercurrent of past and present contributions, subtle and immeasurable, who have made our lives, and the planet's life better. This book is not just about elevating identities of difference to leadership—it is also about elevating the roles that are often devalued, erased, and done by women. We need to hear these stories more often and in more places to feel our power rise so we can connect, embrace hope, feel joy, and make change.

I believe that sharing and listening to our stories can fuel action, connections, and new possibilities. The brave voices, like the ones in this collection, are essential to our survival—together, we are many, and we can change the landscapes of our lives.

What Is EMMA Talks?

carla bergman and Corin Browne

EMMA Talks is a mini–art festival and speakers' series. The core purpose
of EMMA talks is to bring important stories by cis women and two-spirited,
trans, and gender-non-conforming folks who are writers, activists, thinkers,
storytellers, makers, and doers, from the periphery to the public. Together
their stories build a powerful, engaging collection of talks that celebrate
and build on the conversations, imaginings, and hard work of individuals,
communities, and social movements. Below are the core values that under-
scored the project:

EMMA Talks aims to counteract the social silencing of women's stories
and work.

EMMA Talks works to carve out well-deserved spaces for women and
trans folks to share their stories and work with a large, diverse audience.

EMMA means Engaging Monologue Mutual Aid.

Each EMMA Talk begins and ends with a short social gathering, cohosted
by Simon Frasier University's Office for Community Engagement, and
includes a facilitated community-engaged art-making time. This social
gathering and art-making space takes the place of a question and answer
and allows folks to meet one another, converse, and share thoughts about
the talks.

Half of the donations collected through EMMA Talks go to the speaker's
cause or project of choice, while the other half pays tech and support staff.

EMMA Talks, live and online, are professionally produced and accessible. EMMA Talks prioritizes the training of young women and trans folks in tech, including their live camera work and post-production.

The Story of EMMA Talks

carla bergman

EMMA Talks had its genesis in 2011 as I was preparing materials for my seminar class during an alternative to university I co-organized in Vancouver, BC. I wanted to include videos of talks alongside written material and was struck by the scarcity of high-quality videos of cis women, trans women, and gender-nonconforming folks talking about theory and organizing. I was also disappointed to find an overwhelming number of online talks by white cis·men. Institute faculty member Astra Taylor and I, speaking one day, thought it would be amazing to create a version of TED Talks that was more rigorous, fluid, and feminist.

Jump forward three years, and our idea for a public speakers' series was taking hold. In talking with my friend and collaborator Sylvia McFadden about names for the project, and given my long-held love for Emma Goldman, Sylvia immediately suggested I  call the series *Emma*. The name was perfect—Goldman always struck me as having a radiant voice and no fear of using it. I called the series EMMA, meaning Engaging Monologues Mutual Aid, because I wanted, at each event, to invite folks to sit and listen to a monologue.

I had a name and an idea, but I was too busy to start, so onto the back burner it went. Sometimes things have their own inertia, though. A few days later, I met Leanne Betasamosake Simpson and mentioned the EMMA Talks idea. Leanne's immediate excitement made me realize perhaps the time to launch was then.

Then, codirecting a documentary with Corin Browne, a media artist and producer, I brought up EMMA to her, and she immediately said yes. The next hurdle was finding an accessible venue that would offer institutional support to pay both speakers and our team so I could curate with autonomy, so I reached out to friend and colleague Am Johal at SFU Woodwards. Am's enthusiasm and generosity enabled us to start right away. Within a couple months, Corin and I had a website, a logo (by the innovative designer and artist Joi Arcand), an all-female tech crew (too many to name), two charismatic emcees (Tahia Ahmed and later Melanie Matining), a handful of volunteers, a thoughtful access coordinator (Jeanette Sheehy), and the first EMMA booked. EMMA Talks launched with Leanne Betasamosake Simpson and Kian Cham (formally Kelsey C. Corbett) on April 6, 2015.

We early on decided to only produce two or three events a year. In part because EMMA Talks was never an expansive project, it has been one of the most joyful and meaningful projects of my life. As we listened to each other and the community, the project shifted: we added community art engagement and later, in 2016, we added event photographer Vivienne McMaster. In 2017, we commissioned guest curators Tahia Ahmed and Michelle Nahanee to produce their own EMMA Talks. Tahia's was called *Feminist Muslim Voices* and included, alongside a speaker, an onstage dialogue that invited the audience to listen only rather than ask questions, which is commonplace with a panel. Michelle's was called *Messages from Sḵwx̱wú7mesh Matriarchs*. As of the beginning of 2019, EMMA Talks has produced ten events and has an archive of seventeen talks viewed daily around the world—it appears I was not the only one craving this media!

The EMMA team are incredibly grateful for all the love and joy that has gone into making EMMA Talks a success. Thank you to all who took part, especially the volunteers, our partners, and our amazing Tech crew. Our deepest gratitude goes out to the speakers.

CHAPTER ONE

Assemble

(syrinxes)

breath is talking
can you hear me?
What if breath is my second voice?
The song that is moving through
My veins giving life
anticipating
    because
She has so much to say

Is anyone listening?

— carla bergman

Sanibe

Christa Couture

Before I was born, my pregnant mother named me Matthew. She was sure she was having a boy and sure he was a Matthew. When I was born and then gendered a girl, Matthew no longer fit. It took my mom a few days to find an alternative. In 1978, the top girl names in Ontario were Jennifer, Sarah, and Melissa. Eventually, she chose Christa. Christa Faye. She thought it suited me, and she was right.

I have always felt like a Christa—except for a short spell when I was eight and the word *Christa* seemed pointy and sharp. I envied more feminine names and wrote *Christina Rose* repeatedly. I was certain that if I were called Christina Rose, I would possess more grace and girlishness and inhabit my tomboy nature less. My desire was short-lived, though, and soon enough, *Christa* felt comfortable again.

Christa was fine but never Chris, nor any other nickname. My father often said that when I was a child, if someone dared call me "sweetheart" or "pumpkin," I would sternly correct them: "It's *Christa.*" In later years, I would often have to correct those mistaking me for a Kristen or a Crystal. I am much more forgiving now. "There *are* a lot of Chris names," I say. And then I think, *But not many Christas.*

At a summer fair, when I was twelve, I found a booth that would print out the origin and meaning of one's name in a script font onto coloured paper. *Christa. Greek. Anointed one,* said mine. I taped the little paper next to the head of my bed.

I love stories and meanings behind names. I want to know how your name was chosen—for you or how you chose it for yourself. Middle names are often rife with backstory: a beloved great aunt or your parent's first sight on the day of your birth. I have always found these stories irresistible and delightful.

When I was in high school, I would take baby-name books out of the library and hide them under my pillow, worrying that if my mom saw them, she would think I was, or wanted to be, pregnant. Rapt with curiosity and satisfied with the meanings of names, I turned the pages as if they were the best fiction. I looked up the names of everyone I knew. I imagined what people with names I had not yet encountered would be like. I imagined Esmé (French, esteemed, beloved) would be soft-spoken but not shy, observant with round brown eyes. Otis (German, wealthy) would have broad shoulders and strong legs, but despite his body's athletic aptitude, he would be bookish and a little clumsy.

While the story of Christa started with Matthew, I also have another name. My mother is Norwegian and Swedish, and my father was Cree, and when I was two years old, I was given a traditional name. In my Cree culture—in many Indigenous cultures—traditional names are given in ceremony, and they relate to a person's role in the community. The names speak to our gifts and our duty to use those gifts.

My traditional name is Sanibe. SAY-nee-bay. It is not actually a Cree word, because the Elder who gave me my name was Arapaho—we were on his territory, and you work with what you've got. Sanibe means Singing Woman. At my naming ceremony, the Elder, Raymond, told my family, "She's going to sing a lot, and she's going to talk a lot." And *that* story I heard over and over growing up. "Oh, Raymond told us she's going to sing a lot, and she's going to talk a lot . . ." I loved that story, and when that story was told, I felt loved.

As Singing Woman, I have been writing songs for as long as I can remember. For the past fifteen years, I have been recording those songs, performing them on stages across Canada and Europe, and doing my job: being true to my name. Singing songs has not only been my work but also how I have survived the hardest parts of my life. I have experienced a great deal of loss: the loss of my leg to cancer, the loss of my father, the loss of two of my children who died, and the loss of my marriage after that.

I write about these losses in all my songs. By sharing these stories through music, I have felt seen and heard. Grief is a lonely emotion. Yet in moments with audiences, I have felt less alone. "I too lost a son," a woman told me after a show in Winnipeg. "Martin." We hugged, and I promised to remember him. "My husband died last year," I was told during the break at a show in St. John. The woman cried when I gave her a hug. "Walter," he was called. I promised to remember him, too. I learned to focus on only one person at a time when others were waiting to buy my CDs or say hello.

I began dedicating a song every night on stage to the most recent person I had been told about. Most often, they were children who had died. Bereaved parents found me as though they could see me in the dark. (I could see them, too.)

Sometimes these moments of connection did not come from someone else's story but from the wordless magic and suspension of sharing music and feeling the audience with me as I sang. For a long time, until I had new things to hold on to, those moments kept me alive.

Someone asked me recently about the loss of my children: "How are you okay?" It was hard to answer because, like anyone, my emotional state is not fixed. Sometimes I am okay, and sometimes I am not okay, and that is human. But I replied, "Time passing helps, and singing and writing helps." This is the reciprocal part of Sanibe—the name speaks to what I can give, but it has also been a huge part of what I have received.

In 2016, I had two surgeries on my neck: one to remove thyroid cancer and a second to address an arterial bleed that erupted in the first hours of recovery. Those surgeries changed my voice. They changed my singing voice. Once the swelling went down and panic and fear of the bleed subsided, I could still sing. But it was different. My range and capacity had decreased, and for the first time ever, I would, unpredictably, miss notes. My voice, which I had known so intimately, felt like an untamed creature. What, for me, had always been truly inherent, easy, and pleasurable was missing.

My heart ached; I did not recognize myself. Another loss. I stopped performing. I didn't know what to do with the new voice. I resented its limitations, and I was struggling with that reality. *How can I be Singing Woman if I'm not singing songs?*

In 2017, I was invited to perform at an event in Port Hope, Ontario. I knew it was to present my music, but I was not ready to sing in front of people with my new, broken voice. I scheduled a breakfast meeting with the event organizers to talk about options, and as I looked in the mirror before the meeting, the story I had heard so many times came to mind: "She's going to sing a lot, and she's going to talk a lot." And then, too, I remembered: I loved that story, and when that story was told, I felt loved.

I stopped and held my own gaze. For the first time ever, I heard the second half of that teaching. I had always understood "she's going to sing a lot"—that part is obvious. But I always thought "she's going to talk a lot" just meant I was chatty. It suddenly occurred to me "she's going to talk a lot" was also part of being Sanibe and that "talk a lot" could also be part of who I am—my role in the world is how I serve my community. I can *talk*. As I considered this for the first time, I felt a wave of relief.

For my entire adult life, singing has been both my job and the means through which I open my heart and others' hearts. It was the only reason I ever stepped on a stage. On the night of the event, I walked out from the wings, neither guitar in hand nor piano to turn to. This was a first for me.

I approached the mic and blinked at the spotlights. I imagined being greeted with kindness in the silent auditorium. I spoke. My voice hung in the room. I was nervous without the company of an instrument to help fill that space. But I pushed my feet onto the floor and took the same deep breath I always did. I told the ears and hearts there what I had been trying to come to terms with: my voice was injured, I did not know who Sanibe could be anymore, and I was grappling with my identity. I told them I had never spoken like this before. I told them about loss, resilience, and hope. I started moving my arms through the air as I spoke, expressing to the rhythm and cadence of my words, just as I once did on piano. My nervousness subsided, and before my talk was done, I found the bits of silence once filled by instruments to be a beautiful sound.

Speaking to an audience felt raw and new—exciting, too. But it was also familiar. It turns out that stepping up to a mic and sharing can invite listeners just like singing does: they are each an invitation to be less alone.

I am Singing Woman, with or without a song.

Telling a New Story

Tasha Kaur

As with most people who grew up in families that do not fit the mould will understand, I learned from an early age to split myself into different parts. The divide between the me that existed with my Punjabi family and the me that existed at my predominantly white elementary school was stark. When I was in Grade 1, a few white girls in my class asked me if I believed in Jesus. I was confused by the question. I had never been asked that before. Then they asked if I believed in the devil. I did not know who the devil was nor what it meant to believe in him. I eventually told them I did not, but it did not matter. The pause in my response and confusion on my face gave me away as different. I felt hurt and embarrassed. My sister describes these events in our lives as the constant humiliation of being the *other*: the feeling of knowing you have done something to reveal the myriad ways you do not belong.

I was a smart kid, though, and figured out a life hack for this situation. I quickly learned the separate rules for existence: though they were only a five-minute walk from each other, home and school had different languages, foods, and ways of being. I figured out how to be normal and acceptable at school: don't talk about your non-christian god, don't speak Punjabi, ignore it when someone is confused by you living with your grandparents, aunts, and uncles. I studied whiteness and became good at appealing to it. But I shed that way of being when I got home. Quite literally as soon as I walked into my house after school, I would go straight to my room and change into my home clothes. I performed the two separate parts of myself with such ease that even I did not notice when I switched. It was only when my two worlds collided that I felt jarring discomfort, as if a secret was being revealed.

When I was eight, I injured my toe playing at home and developed a slight limp when I walked. My grandmother, loving as she was, thought I would have trouble walking home for lunch that day, so she brought my lunch to school. She showed up in my classroom doorway dressed in a brightly patterned Punjabi suit, carrying my lunch in steel dishes on a metal tray with a large steel jug of milk covered in tinfoil. All my classmates ate white-bread sandwiches from Ziploc bags. I rushed to the door and told her in Punjabi that we had to go home. I was upset at her for coming to school. She did not understand why and thought I was being so strange for not wanting to eat at school. I could not explain I did not want her looking like that in my school. I made up an excuse—I cannot remember what. I still worry she felt rejected. I did, after all, reject her in that moment, her offering of love and care and what she revealed about who I am. These kinds of betrayals come from the impossible dance of hiding half of yourself.

From this early age, like so many women of colour, I learned how to read the expectations others would set out for me and meet them. This was how I tried to be "good" and make people happy. I was, for the most part, a "good" daughter and granddaughter at home. And I was a "good" normal kid at school. This early training of putting others before myself has never left me.

It is not all bad. In fact, there are many aspects of this characteristic I quite like. In our hyper-individualist capitalist world, being conditioned to think about others helped quiet the *me first* voice that might have otherwise taken over. There is much value in putting others first. I like that I grew up with a practice that says hosts only eat after all their guests are well fed. Or that even as a kid, I was expected to check if any grandparents, especially those with mobility or health issues, needed food before I served myself. While I did not understand it this way at the time, an analysis of power underscores this behaviour. If I am a young, able-bodied person, of course I should check with older members of the community and help them get their needs met first.

As I grew older, I learned more about power and justice. I was drawn to justice work. The intimacy of being the other has served me well in this area, too. While I hold privileges of class, citizenship, able-bodied-ness, a cisgender identity, and being a settler, my life in this marginalized body has helped me stay present with what it means to be betrayed by allies I thought I could trust. I know what it feels like to think it would be easier for everyone if I could just keep my emotions to myself—be quiet, go along with the crowd, let myself be erased. I carry that pain and do my best to avoid enacting that violence on others. Even though I have fucked up, I put a great deal of intention into being in solidarity with people whose struggles are different from mine.

I am far from perfect in this journey, and I am committed to learning and growing. I recognize that this learning and growth comes from people who have trusted me with their struggles, and I hope to live up to that honour. I have been fortunate enough to take on leadership roles in communities and organizations working for social justice—we are all leaders, but I am referring to ones acknowledged by hierarchies. Even within those positions, I have been happy to stay in the background. In part, this comes from a healthy intent to be mindful of my privilege. I try to ask: *Is there someone whose voice is more important here?* Part of this motivation, though, comes from a less healthy comfort I find in hiding. Speaking in public is not personal for me. It is about supporting a community, campaign, or direct action against injustice. It is not *this* story—me and the details of my life. That is something I reserve for intimate conversations in small rooms without cameras and an audience of strangers.

Writing this piece was deeply frightening. I fear being an imposter. I fear revealing this much of me so publicly. I have been told I am a good storyteller. I know how to combine humour, drama, and vulnerability to tell a story that is entertaining. For most of my stories, I calculate how vulnerable I want to be—just enough to make me authentic but not so much I feel scared. While many social spaces claim to value authenticity, we fail to recognize that the ability to be honest is a privilege. The more privileged and valued you are by society, the less cost there is being yourself. If you have this kind of privilege, you know what it means to be desired—social media and social capital amplify what is desirable. The authentic is not easily separated from a selective performance of authenticity. I cannot say for sure where this story sits on that spectrum.

Writing this story was unbelievably challenging. I had to push myself to stop thinking about what other people want to hear and start thinking about what I need to say. Thinking about what I need is like using a muscle that has atrophied after a long period of lack of use. Writing this story required new kinds of vulnerability and admitting things I have never talked about. It involved taking up space I am not sure belongs to me—space just for my benefit. I take comfort in the idea that this is an experiment: I am trying something new, a new way of being. I am unsure if it will be a permanent change, but I am glad to have taken the risk. I also take comfort in knowing that my vision of justice includes many more people taking up space with their untold stories. I want to hear their stories. Meaningful relationships require reciprocity. This essay is my offering to all the courageous storytellers. I hope to hear more of your voices.

We Owe Each Other Kindness

Kinnie Starr

THE PRACTICE OF KINDNESS

I have been professionally writing beats and songs since 1996. I write
mainly about society, community, water, and identity, and I would say I
write more questions than answers. I am not an expert on human behaviour,
but I am a curious person who has made a living from observation, and I
am interested in becoming a better person. We all have the potential to
be our best selves—by which I mean our kindest selves, radiating from
generous centres.

I think a lot about this stuff—about kindness, about home. I always have.
I am interested in how we are each made of many parts. I have noticed we
can all be unkind at times; this is part of who we are as whole and flawed
beings. We can also be kind, coming from a warm place that wishes others
and ourselves well. I believe the practice of being kind, or love-ing, grounds
us and returns us home, to a place of sovereignty.

I have always researched love and kindness to study how to relate better
to others. I like learning about this stuff because I want to improve as a
human being. I am also recovering from a vehicle accident that chronically
injured my body, so I want to reduce pain. And serotonin, produced inter-
nally through acts of good will, is a damn good start.

Two years ago, I was in fighting shape, mentally and physically, preparing for far-reaching and meaningful projects—some of which are now out in the world. And then I was in a taxi accident that derailed me. Since then, my body has unravelled. My stomach and reproductive system fell apart first. I got my period for eight months straight and then stopped bleeding altogether, and my digestive tract was on fire for over a year, making absorption of nutrients impossible as food would move through me at lightning speed. My spatial reasoning, cognition, and reading ability changed, and I needed surgery on my upper back at my T4 vertebrae. My hips and groin stopped working well, my comprehension went downhill, my irritability and emotions ping ponged around, and as anyone who has experienced a traumatic brain injury can relate to, I generally stopped feeling like myself. My senses amplified: I became unnaturally sensitive to sound, smells, light, and movement. I grew afraid of vehicles and was filled with *dis*-ease. My new state of chronic pain, coupled with the fallout from head trauma, put me in a tailspin of negativity. I became hyperaware of unkindness, both directed at and coming from me.

During this time period, a peer suggested to me that nobody owes anyone any kindness. Her viewpoint impacted me for a few sad days. *She is right,* I thought. *The world is hard and competitive; we do not owe each other any kindness—I just need a tougher skin.*

But I don't have tough skin, not even close. I am a softie, and I've made a living off of being that way, being vulnerable publicly while trying to articulate contradictory worldviews. And with being a public figure comes envy and hatred but also applause and support, depending, I suppose, on who is observing me and what is going on in their life.

Being a public figure at times offers undue adoration, which seems unfitting, because I am an asshole, but then again so is everyone. Put your hand up, please, if you have never been a jerk, never started or been drawn into gossip, never treated someone poorly, and never done something wrong. Life is complicated and challenging, and we are all navigating the world as best we can. We all stumble, we all get hurt, and we all hurt each other. But is that a reason not to practise kindness? Does the complicated terrain of being alive mean we all have carte blanche to treat others poorly? Do we need tougher skins to justify being bigger jerks, expecting others to be tougher too, or do we need softer skins that enable us to be more vulnerable and gentle, soliciting the same from others? I'm not calling kindness a practice for nothing. You need to practise until you are good at it. Then you need to keep practising until it becomes second nature.

KINDNESS IN AN INTERNET ERA

Our cues for how to behave come from many sources: each other, language and print, families, work environments, TV, the Internet, and social media. I would argue that most of us (myself included) spend too much time consciously and unconsciously modelling ourselves on media cues. We deal with a lot of external forces through the influence of media—print, TV, and the web. The mainstreaming of media-endorsed behaviour can take us away from our best selves—the home inside of us.

I grew up in Calgary, Alberta, in a house full of boys. My brothers were very social people and so were my parents. My brothers and father, and the friends they had over regularly, glued themselves to the television non-stop. Looking back, I recall them and people in general loving shows like *Seinfeld*, *The Cosby Show*, *The Facts of Life*, *Fresh Prince*, *Three's Company*, and *The Brady Bunch*. These shows focused on human relationships rather than competition, getting famous, and calling each other out. Sure there were competitive shows in the eighties, too—*Wheel of Fortune*, *Jeopardy!* and of course sports—but the whole North American reality TV modality of shaming each other, inciting drama, and gossiping wasn't a central part of programming then like it is now. According to a UCLA study, community feeling in 1987 was ranked number one in on-screen TV values. Soon after, community dropped to number eleven, replaced by the pursuit of fame, which between 1987 and 2007 became the number one television-programming value. When you look around, it resonates: seeking fame, money, calling others out in fits of righteousness, winning, trolling and shaming are still mainstream TV values today, with people emulating the culture they consume. Of course there's great TV programming out there too, and I have hope for more written and produced content that is passionate about focusing on connection between people.

Beyond TV, the abundance of gossip magazines (which encourage mean and competitive thinking like who got uglier, who has the most cellulite and why it's bad, who went crazy) are part of that same core value system and throwaway behaviour and those magazines are everywhere, at least in North America: gas stations, airports, grocery stores, dental offices, hairdressers, and drugstores—*everywhere*. This messaging impacts how we think about the world. How could it not? It encourages us to be selfish, competitive, and unkind.

When I make this assertion, I'm looking at mainstream pop culture. There are hundreds of shows, podcasts, magazines, books, and websites that do not support seeking fame, winning, and putting people down as ultimate life goals. I am encouraged by the growth of informative, kind-spirited, educational programming that emphasizes connection between people. It gives me hope for us all.

Let's shift the lens off of TV and gossip magazines and onto the Internet, which is the way that most of us consume information and behavioural coding in today's screen-obsessed culture. The pursuit of fame and the accumulation of followers and 'likes' are central goals we are encouraged to pursue. Professional artists supply their YouTube, Twitter, and Instagram accounts with frantic creative output (however banal) to stay atop viewers' newsfeeds. This is supposedly one of the most important parts of "building your brand." I am not sure this relentless courting of attention and numbers does much to improve our internal wellness, though. The pursuit of visibility, though commercially paramount from a business perspective, has a dark side. If you have no traction, you feel like a loser. And if you have traction, you can elicit jealousy and hatred for being successful.

I'm aware of the Internet's value. The Internet and the digital exchange of information has been a powerful connector in solving crimes, organizing political actions, bringing awareness to marginalized folks like trans and displaced people, and reconnecting separated refugee families. The Internet can be an amazing place! There are enough viral videos of puppies, kitties, and bunnies chasing away bears to show we are softies at heart.

Here in North America, we are heavy media consumers. At our worst, we copy the behaviour we see daily. We consume content that teaches us getting even is better than being charitable. We have grown to believe it's fine to text or e-mail the meanest taunts simply by virtue of having communication at our fingertips at any moment of any day. Divorcees and jilted lovers are taught that ruining an ex's life is a game to be won. "Revenge, revenge, revenge! You go, girl!" Some of us, especially when riddled by jealousy, an emotion encouraged in dominant culture, troll pages to aggressively put others in their place. When something bad happens to another person, we gloat and spread demeaning memes, claiming they had it coming.

Kindness in an Internet era is therefore critical because the virtual space once considered separate from the real world now pervades existence. We are in a flood of immediacy and our careless communications show it: we urgently perform, compete, and stay on top of feeds, e-mails, texts, and posts by any means. Inside virtual space, strangers or ill-intentioned peers have intimate access to others' lives. This anonymity can be a dangerous playground for our darkest natures.

Why do we do this? What do we gain by putting others down, by enjoying others' ill fortune, or attempting to speedily demean others? What is the difference between pointing out another person's faults with the intent to empower them and doing the same to unravel them? Can we answer these questions? Can we head towards kindness despite the tone of media we digest? Can we return inward toward personal sovereignty, away from homogenized behaviour, toward home?

HEADING HOME

What exactly is kindness? For me the practice of kindness can be broken down into ongoing and active methodologies. I think being kind is the active pursuit of empowering someone rather than destabilizing them. Making someone feel valued and cared for can be as simple as communicating clearly, not confusing or derailing, not sending texts or rants meant to unsettle, and not filling someone with dread, guilt, or self-doubt. It means choosing to communicate from a place of good intention rather than with intent to unhinge, belittle, or traumatize.

Kindness can also be a giving of hard truths. I include teasing and comedy in this action—teasing, through laughter, can make another person feel part of a group. Of course, teasing can be malicious too, so I suppose I am returning back to the idea of coming from a warm centre with the intention of making someone feel included and help them laugh at themselves. This is a different thing than teasing with the intention to humiliate rather than include. I think we recognize the former from the latter. We build community and personal sovereignty by practicing the former. Ultimately, it is our agency that defines our intention.

To be clear, when I talk about kindness, I am not talking about niceness—certainly not a protocolled or Eurocentric definition of politeness or manners. Politeness can actually restrict people, especially given what is considered polite varies so much from community to community. I am also not talking about the kindness of a box of chocolates given to receive something back.

The interesting part of this conversation is that the practice of kindness is not necessarily selfless, as being kind is a way to increase our health. Being kind has positive neurological benefits. Acts of generosity release serotonin into the brain and reduce the stress hormone cortisol. Acting from a place of care soothes our nerves because gentleness produces endorphins, nature's painkiller, in the brain. Many of us need to love our nervous systems, which are tattered by life, injury, media, sensationalized news, work, and the overabundance of information we digest each time we open our computers or walk down a street. Acts of generosity also produce oxytocin, known as 'the cuddle hormone.' Compassionate people have more DHEA, the hormone that slows aging. Those who use Instagram filters to smooth their complexions might reduce their wrinkles just by loving more!

Kindness is an action in the sense that when we practise it, we extend ourselves for the betterment of others and ourselves. Kindness as self-care helps us feel more at home and centred in our bodies. This can include getting enough sleep, spending time with people who love us, leaving toxic relationships and behaviours behind, eating food with higher nutritional value when possible, allowing ourselves to take time off, and taking time to immerse ourselves in the natural world.

I know for me, this is important. As I have said, I can be both a jerk and a softie. I am a contradiction walking around in a broken body. I'm no more or less important than anyone else. I'm bacteria, blood, water, calcium, and questions. I'm nobody. But I'm somebody, too. And aren't we all nobody? Aren't we all somebody? If we are all nobody and somebody in a sea of nobodies and somebodies, we become everybody. And in that sea of everybody, we are humanity.

The root of the word *kindness* is *kin*—meaning we are all connected. To think of ourselves as connected suggests we do in fact owe each other kindness, because every positive intention or action can create a similar output in an interconnected world.

So, although my peer briefly convinced me that kindness between people is not necessary, I refuse to embrace that view. I know I'm not alone. I see people reject meanness and competitiveness all the time. I look for gentleness and I find it. It's there in all of us if we choose to share it. So what if instead of looking at the world and ourselves in such a manner that nobody owes anybody any kindness, what if instead all we owe each other is kindness?

How do we make kindness part of life? We embrace it like any movement—not a movement with a fancy acronym, a clubhouse, or a beer fridge, and not a movement heavily covered by the media, but a movement in which we know its members: the kind among us. We join them. We reward them. We appreciate their kindnesses, and we forgive their transgressions. We model the good we see in people so that others may see the good in us.

And in that way we become a part of a snowball; a rolling, growing, bright and active momentum.

Trust me, I'm not at the centre of this. I am at the outer edges of this snowball. The outer layer that still runs into all the garbage, the little bits of rock, twigs, and bottle caps from the ground. But as this snowball, this propulsion of kindness, grows and builds, I try to reattach to the goodness inside myself that comes from the home that is mine alone, unaffected by outside forces. And I believe we can all do this. And then I will be insulated by kindness in my community. And, in turn, I will insulate you.

On the Last Leg of the Journey:
An Interview with Helen Hughes

carla bergman

In thinking about *Radiant Voices* and voice generally—who has voice, who is listened to, and who is left out—I thought of Helen Hughes, my dear friend and one of my most important long-term mentors. To have a voice, you must have a listener. Helen is the person in my life who does this profound listening. She is always curious and open. Helen gave me voice, and I am forever grateful. She has given hundreds of others voice, too.

Helen co-created Windsor House, an alternative K-to-12 school in North Vancouver, back in the early seventies. For the past forty-eight years, she has been the matriarch of this democratically run school–community. The number of people who benefited from Helen is impossible to determine: it includes not just students, staff, and families directly involved at Windsor House, but also all who those folks encountered—the ripple effect is immense and truly awe-inspiring.

Here is my conversation with Helen about voice and listening.

Why and how did you get involved in education?

My parents were teachers, and my home life was secure. I spent my blissful teen years with my dog Topper in the wilds of Mosquito Creek in North Vancouver. I somehow blocked out my schooling—I was very good at seeming to pay attention while being somewhere else entirely. Adulthood came as a rude awakening. Just nineteen, I married, started teaching—forty-five students to a class in those days—and tried to learn how to shop, cook, and clean, as well as work full time. I came up short in all categories. That is when my education truly started.

The first thing I learned was to notice what people were actually saying. I learned a lot from my students. When my daughter balked strenuously at going to school in Grade 2, I got together with some other parents and started a school in my house. We knew what we didn't want but had no clear picture of what we did want. The school wobbled along—with the fifteen children playing, making use of the many things available to them, while the parents talked endlessly about the philosophy of learning and teaching. We all read every book that came along. Summerhill was our role model. After four years, we could no longer manage privately, so we asked the North Vancouver School District to take us in, which they did. Alternative schools were all the rage in those days. Windsor House, so named because it started in a house on Windsor Road, grew and thrived. Eventually we had two hundred students, and I was made vice principal. My three children attended Windsor House, and now my grandchildren do as well. They are all fine people, so freedom can work if it suits your style.

Helen, you have always been part of educational projects and movements. Can you tell us some of the things you learned most from this work?

I thought, when I turned seventy-five, that I would just coast to the end. I'd lived a great life—felt joy, excruciating remorse, grief, a great deal of pleasure, and a lot of just managing from one day to the next. I worked hard and played hard, and now I could take it easy. How wrong I was! There is no rest for the curious, so I am careening down the last run of the rollercoaster—with my hair flying, my eyes wide open, and my ears perked. What I have learned most from this work is that listening to understand is completely different from listening to make a clever rebuttal.

What is next on the horizon for you?

I decided to spend what is possibly the last fifteen years of my life finding out who I am. I discovered, of course, that I keep changing, so I never really get a handle on it. Also, since I am so embedded in my culture, it's hard to know what is the essence of me and what is the result of conditioning. I'm still curious about it but no longer see it as something I can actually complete. So now I'm hankering for one last project—something that I can manage, something simple, something where I won't be letting people down as I become more doddering and forgetful.

I love that distinction of being part of culture—to know where you start and where the culture ends is challenging for any of us. Do you have any ideas on what that next project might be?

Well, what are my strengths? I don't cook worth a damn, nor clean, nor garden, nor exercise, nor shop. Hmm. What I enjoy and what I do well is observe people and listen, in order to understand. As a result of this, I notice patterns. One of these patterns is that when people are in conflict and when they start to try to reason with each other, they often use reasons as weapons. They just keep coming up with reasons and counter reasons, and eventually the strongest, richest, loudest person wins, leaving the other person resentful. I rarely see someone say, "Oh, I see your point! Of course, you are right. Let's do it your way."

Reasons are so seductive, though. Check out this link, watch this video, read this quote—then surely, you will agree with me! This popular person, brilliant thinker, renowned scientist says this, so it must be true. It is very unusual to come across someone who is willing to set aside reasons in order to come to mutually agreeable solutions. I am of the opinion that there must be something better.

I agree—there has got to be a better way! I really like the idea of not using reason this way. Can you provide some examples?

My life's work has made it possible for me to have many young friends, and I noticed that among the young people that I hang out with brainstorming seems more effective than sweet reason. The explanation for this is that it is hard for most humans to actually listen to another person's reasoning because half of their brain is busy coming up with a rebuttal. If you are brainstorming, however—just throwing out ideas with no need to favour any particular one—then you can actually hear a suggestion that might appeal to you. Or you hear a suggestion that would work with a minor tweak. At that point, you are both on the same team, trying to create a solution that is good enough to try. Each suggestion should start with words like *I have an idea*, *My suggestion is*, *How about we try*, *Could we*. All suggestions are okay. If you don't like one, then just ignore it. When you hear one you sort of like, then you can add to it with improvements.

For older folk, it is much the same: suggestions only, no negation of suggestions, no suggestions of reason or fairness, just possible ideas. The tentative solution need not be bulletproof; it just has to be worth trying. I have an example from today: My grandchildren arrived in a squabbling mood. I intervened. I said that if they were going to be on each other's nerves I would put them in different rooms while I got lunch, and then we could do something together. They clearly didn't want to be separated, so they both chimed in with good will. The eldest had built a fort in the living room and had used two giant padded boppers as door posts. He didn't want his sister to play in his fort. The youngest suggested that they share the boppers. The eldest said no. I reminded them that the best brainstorming is without negation. If they don't like a suggestion, just ignore it.

The next suggestion was for the eldest to carry on in his fort and the youngest to help with lunch—then, in quick succession:
- Hop around the house on one foot;
- Cooperate in the fort;
- Eldest play in the fort and youngest have candies;

- All make lunch together;
- Eldest get the living room and youngest eat grapes while I make lunch;
- Make lunch with feet tied together including me—I had a good laugh at this one, which raised the goodwill of the brainstorming;
- Eldest get the living room and the dining room and youngest get playroom and study;
- Play separately in the same room without bugging; make a fire in the fireplace and watch it.

Unfortunately, the word *watch* sounded a bit like *wash*, so the eldest said if we wash the fire, then it will go out. He was attempting humour, but it seemed like a put-down, so the energy dropped. I commended the joke and noted that the energy had dropped

Then I suggested one outside and one inside. The energy was wobbling, and we were all hungry, so I resorted to a bulletproof idea that one could use my iPad and the other my iPhone. The eldest picked that up, but the youngest was, to my amazement, unmoved. I was getting hungry myself, so I went back to an old suggestion with a new twist. I suggested that we all make lunch together, but we could walk only on the green squares of the kitchen tiles. By then they were ready to settle. The suggestion by the youngest that the eldest run up and down the stairs while she counted was enthusiastically agreed upon. Go figure!

Why do you think it works?

I am puzzled by the apparent success of this rather odd method and wonder if it can be put to greater use. I recognize that some matters are actually life or death and that running up and down the stairs is not going to help. However, I do believe that in all disputes, things are either going to stay the same or they are going to change. Given that truism, it seems like a good idea to employ a style that is wide open and without judgments to at least find temporary solutions and at best make incremental changes to keep things from becoming too rigid to survive changing conditions.

This model gives voice and power to everyone involved. I think you have an incredible ability to remain curious and to trust both the people around you and the process. How did you learn these skills? Why is listening so important?

Back in the day when I was fostering young people, we had ample opportunity to try out some of these ideas. My favourite story was about one young person who always left the teapot dirty. When I went to use it, I had to wash it first. We tried this system then that system, but all of them failed. Finally, in a burst of brilliance, my boarder said, "Why don't we *both* not wash the pot when we are finished with it. Then we only need to wash it just before we use it." I was dumbfounded. My stance was so righteous and hers was so clearly wrong that it took a few moments while I processed the idea and realized it could work really well! Sure enough, when I washed the pot before I used it, the pot was warm as well as clean.

When I tell this story to a group of adults, they are often shocked. Some absolutely will not agree that it was a good solution. Somehow it offends a deep moral obligation to always clean up after yourself! This idea of right or fair gets in the way a lot.

What else gets in the way of people being able to approach decisions this way?

When I was at Hollyhock this summer, they had just issued a ruling that the hot tubs were no longer bathing suit optional. There was grumbling. I said to one gentleman, "Why don't you ask if you can work out a solution with them?" "How could you do that?" he said, "Either you're naked or you're not—there is no compromise possible." I was astonished. "There are many different options—have different hours for different dress codes; have one hot tub optional and the other bathing suits required; build a screen between the two pools; wear blindfolds; make a tent to put over one; have days on and days off; have times for different sexes, different ages, different moral codes; turn off all the lighting." He was unmoved. I realize that my worldview includes casting about for unusual solutions for seemingly intractable problems. I don't see things as either this or that. I see the world as a place of outrageously improbable solutions that astoundingly work.

Yes, I often say what about options three, four, five, and six? I am pretty sure I gained the ability to ask these questions from being around you. I like what you are saying here. It feels deeply relational, and it makes me think about collaboration. How does collaboration fit into this model?

Well, it's an informal method of collaboration and can be done by almost anyone. When children have been supported to be successful using informal collaboration, they can do it easily and quickly by themselves in their day-to-day lives. More formal collaboration, however, can only be done by people of good will. It is only effective when meetings are run by a person who can hold everyone to an agreement. The agreement needs to be one of only coming up with ideas, with no spoken or physically indicated rejection. When the felt sense of the meeting moves the moderator to ask if all can agree to try a solution, there may be tweaking of the favourite suggestion to make it acceptable to all. Then comes raised hands to show agreement to support the solution for a given length of time. I notice that I have used the term only three times in one paragraph. I am wary of using absolutes, so I am open to revisiting this.

How do you see this in relation to the question of radical social change?

I remember being told that in any grouping—people, villages, algae—there had to be about eighty percent of the entities that stayed the same down through time and twenty percent that changed. This was to keep the organism from becoming too rigid to accommodate changing conditions or from becoming too flexible to hold together. This idea made me much more appreciative of all of the rigid systems that hinder the implementation of my wild fancies. Nonetheless, I am very grateful for those folks who get out there and insist on change. You are the ones who get squished and maligned, but you are the ones who will save the day.

If you had one piece of advice to give to those of us who want to see social change in the world, what would it be?

My advice would be to support one another. If the group you are in heads in a direction you don't want to go, leave. Find a more compatible group or start one of your own. Do not put sand in the gears of a machine that is working. In my lifetime, I have seen many worthwhile groups implode while fighting with one another over insignificant details. Oddly enough, this seems to be a more left-wing issue than a right-wing one. The Right seems more capable of coming up with simplistic ideologies that tap into visceral support, while the Left seems to want to fine-tune to perfection before going into action.

When you find a group that you like, appreciate the work of others in your group, use goodwill to understand different ideas, turn criticisms into suggestions, and don't break into secret groups. If you think someone should do something differently, then model how effective your method is. Move toward the trouble—it rarely goes away on its own. Talk with the person you understand the least and listen closely so that you can explain their position with grace. I want to be clear that I do not oppose militancy. There are some groups that need to be stopped. The KKK comes to mind. I'll leave it to you young people to find ingenious ways to fight intolerance and greed.

On the Meaning of 'Gossip'

Silvia Federici

Tracing the history of the words frequently used to define and degrade women is a necessary step if we are to understand how gender oppression functions and reproduces itself. The history of 'gossip' is emblematic in this context. Through it we can follow two centuries of attacks on women at the dawn of modern England, when a term commonly indicating a close female friend turned into one signifying idle, backbiting talk—that is, talk potentially sowing discord, the opposite of the solidarity that female friendship implies and generates. Attaching a denigrating meaning to the term indicating friendship among women served to destroy the female sociality that had prevailed in the Middle Ages, when most of the activities women performed were of a collective nature and, in the lower classes at least, women formed a tight-knit community that was the source of a strength unmatched in the modern era.

Traces of the use of the word are frequent in the literature of the period. Deriving from the Old English terms God and sibb (akin), 'gossip' originally meant 'god-parent,' one who stands in a spiritual relation to the child to be baptized. In time, however, the term was used with a broader meaning. In early modern England the word 'gossip' referred to companions in childbirth not limited to the midwife. It also became a term for women friends with no necessary derogatory connotations.[1] In either case, it had strong emotional connotations. We recognize it when we see the word in action, denoting the ties that bound women in premodern English society.

We find a particular example of this connotation in a mystery play of the Chester Cycle, suggesting that 'gossip' was a term of strong attachment. Mystery plays were the product of guild members, who by creating and financing these representations tried to boost their social standing as part of the local power structure.[2] Thus, they were committed to upholding expected forms of behavior and satirizing those to be condemned. They were critical of strong, independent women, and especially of their relations to their husbands, to whom—the accusation went—they preferred their friends. As Thomas Wright reports in *A History of Domestic Manners and Sentiments in England during the Middle Ages* (1862),[3] they frequently depicted them as conducting a separate life, often "assembling with their 'gossips' in public taverns to drink and amuse themselves." Thus, in one of the mystery plays of the Chester Cycle representing Noah urging people and animals to enter the ark, the wife is shown sitting in the tavern with her 'gossips' and refusing to leave when the husband calls for her, even as the waters are rising, "unless she is allowed to take her gossips with her."[4] These, as reported by Wright, are the words that she was made to utter by the (clearly disapproving) mystery's author:

> Yes, Sir, set up your sail,
> And row forth with evil hail,
> for without fail,
> I will not out of this town,
> But I have my gossips, everyone,
> One foot further I will not go.
> They will not drown, by St. John
> And I may save their lives!
> They love me full well, by Christ!
> But you let them into your boat,
> Otherwise row now where you like
> And get yourself a new wife.[5]

In the play the scene ends with a physical fight in which the wife beats the husband.

"The tavern," Wright points out, "was the resort of women of the middle and lower orders who assembled there to drink and gossip." He adds: "The meetings of gossips in taverns form the subjects of many of the popular songs of the fifteenth and sixteenth centuries, both in England and France."[6] As an example, he cites a song, possibly from the middle of the fifteenth century, that describes one of these meetings. The women here, "having met accidentally," decide to go "where the wine is best," two by two to not attract attention and be detected by their husbands.[7] Once arrived, they praise the wine and complain about their marital situations. Then they go home, by different streets, "telling their husbands that they had been to church."[8]

The literature of mysteries and morality plays belongs to a period of transition in which women still maintained a considerable degree of social power, but their social position in urban areas was increasingly under threat, as the guilds (that sponsored the production of the plays) were beginning to exclude them from their ranks and institute new boundaries between the home and public space. Not surprisingly, then, women in them were often chastised and represented as quarrelsome, aggressive, and ready to give battle to their husbands. Typical of this trend was the representation of the 'battle for the breeches,' where the woman appeared as the dominatrix—whipping her husband, straddling across his back, in a reversal of role clearly intended to shame men for allowing their wives to be 'on the top.'[9]

These satirical representations, expressions of a growing misogynous sentiment, were instrumental to the politics of the guilds that were striving to become exclusively male preserves. But the representation of women as strong, self-asserting figures also captured the nature of the gender relations of the time, for neither in rural nor urban areas were women dependent on men for their survival; they had their own activities and shared much of their lives and work with other women. Women cooperated with each other in every aspect of their life. They sewed, washed their clothes, and gave birth surrounded by other women, with men rigorously excluded from the chamber of the delivering one. Their legal status reflected this greater autonomy. In Italy in the fourteenth century they could still go independently to court to denounce a man if he assaulted or molested them.[10]

By the sixteenth century, however, women's social position had begun to deteriorate, satire giving way to what without exaggeration can be described as a war on women, especially of the lower classes, reflected in the increasing number of attacks on women as 'scolds' and domineering wives and of witchcraft accusations.[11] Along with this development, we begin to see a change in the meaning of gossip, increasingly designating a woman engaging in idle talk.

The traditional meaning lingered on. In 1602, when Samuel Rowlands wrote *Tis Merrie When Gossips Meete*, a satirical piece describing three London women spending hours in a tavern talking about men and marriages, the word was still used to signify female friendships, implying that "women could create their social networks and their own social space" and stand up to male authority.[12] But as the century progressed the word's negative connotation became the prevalent one. As mentioned, this transformation went hand in hand with the strengthening patriarchal authority in the family and women's exclusion from the crafts and guilds,[13] which, combined with the process of enclosures, led to a "feminization of poverty."[14] With the consolidation of the family and male authority within it, representing the power of the state with regard to wives and children, and with the loss of access to former means of livelihood both women's power and female friendships were undermined.

Thus, while in the Late Middle Ages a wife could still be represented as standing up to her husband and even coming to blows with him, by the end of the sixteenth century she could be severely punished for any demonstration of independence and any criticism she made against him. Obedience— as the literature of the time constantly stressed—was a wife's first duty, enforced by the Church, the law, public opinion, and ultimately by the cruel punishments that were introduced against the 'scolds,' like the 'scold's bridle,' also called the 'branks,' a sadistic contraption made of metal and leather that would tear the woman's tongue if she attempted to talk. This was an iron framework that enclosed the woman's head. A bridle bit about two inches long and one inch wide projected into the mouth and pressed down on top of the tongue; frequently it was studded with spikes so that if the offender moved her tongue it inflicted pain and made speaking impossible.

First recorded in Scotland in 1567, this torture instrument was designed as a punishment for women of the lower classes deemed 'nags' or 'scolds' or riotous, who were often suspected of witchcraft. Wives who were seen as witches, shrews, and scolds were also forced to wear it locked onto their heads.[15] It was often called the 'gossip bridle,' testifying to the change in the meaning of term. With such a frame locking their heads and mouth, those accused could be led through town in a cruel public humiliation that must have terrified all women, showing what one could expect if she did not remain subservient. Significantly, in the United States, it was used to control slaves in Virginia until the eighteenth century.

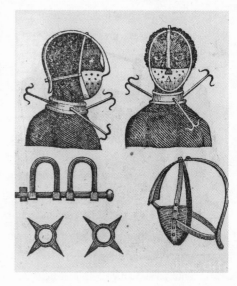

Another torture to which assertive/rebellious women were subjected was the 'cucking stool,' or 'ducking stool,'[16] also used as a punishment for prostitutes and for women taking part in anti-enclosure riots. This was a sort of chair to which a woman was tied and "seated to be ducked in a pond or river." According to D.E. Underdown, "after 1560 evidence of its adoption begins to multiply."[17]

Women were also brought to court and fined for 'scolding,' while priests in their sermons thundered against their tongues. Wives especially were expected to be quiet, "obey their husband without question" and "stand in awe of them." Above all they were instructed to make their husbands and their homes the centers of their attentions and not spend time at the window or at the door. They were even discouraged from paying too many

visits to their families after marriage, and above all from spending
time with their female friends.
Then, in 1547, "a proclamation was
issued forbidding women to meet
together to babble and talk" and
ordering husbands to "keep their
wives in their houses."[18] Female
friendships were one of the

targets of the witch hunts, as in the course of the trials accused women were
forced under torture to denounce each other, friends turning in friends,
daughters turning in their mothers. It was in this context that 'gossip' turned
from a word of friendship and affection into a word of denigration and ridicule. Even when used with the older meaning it displayed new connotations,
referring in the late sixteenth century to an informal group of women who
enforced socially acceptable behavior by means of private censure or public
rituals, suggesting that (as in the case of the midwives) cooperation among
women was being put at the service of upholding the social order.

GOSSIPING AND THE FORMATION OF A FEMALE VIEWPOINT

Gossip today designates informal talk, often damaging to those that are its
object. It is mostly talk that draws its satisfaction from an irresponsible
disparaging of others; it is circulation of information not intended for the
public ear but capable of ruining people's reputations, and it is unequivo-
cally 'women's talk.' It is women who 'gossip,' presumably having nothing
better to do and having less access to real knowledge and information and
a structural inability to construct factually based, rational discourses. Thus,
gossip is an integral part of the devaluation of women's personality and
work, especially domestic work, reputedly the ideal terrain on which this
practice flourishes.

This conception of 'gossip,' as we have seen, emerged in a particular
historical context. Viewed from the perspective of other cultural traditions,

this 'idle women's talk' would actually appear quite different. In many parts of the world, women have historically been seen as the weavers of memory—those who keep alive the voices of the past and the histories of the communities, who transmit them to the future generations and, in so doing, create a collective identity and profound sense of cohesion. They are also those who hand down acquired knowledges and wisdoms—concerning medical remedies, the problems of the heart, and the understanding of human behavior, starting with that of men. Labeling all this production of knowledge 'gossip' is part of the degradation of women—it is a continuation of the demonologists' construction of the stereotypical woman as prone to malignity, envious of other people's wealth and power, and ready to lend an ear to the Devil. It is in this way that women have been silenced and to this day excluded from many places where decisions are taken, deprived of the possibility of defining their own experience, and forced to cope with men's misogynous or idealized portraits of them. But we are regaining our knowledge. As a woman recently put it in a meeting on the meaning of witchcraft, the magic is: "We know that we know."

....

Excerpted from Witches, Witch-Hunting, and Women *by Silvia Federici. Copyright ©* *2018 by Silvia Federici. Reprinted by permission of PM Press.*

Notes

1. Oxford English Dictionary: 'A familiar acquaintance, friend, chum,' supported by references from 1361 to 1873.

2. Nicole R. Rice and Margaret Aziza Pappano, *The Civic Cycles: Artisan Drama and Identity in Premodern England* (Notre Dame, IN: University of Notre Dame Press, 2015).

3. Thomas Wright, *A History of Domestic Manners and Sentiments in England During the Middle Ages* (London: Chapman and Hall, 1862).

4. On the Noah's play in the Chester Cycle, see Rice and Pappano, The Civic Cycles, 165–84.

5. Wright, *A History of Domestic Manners and Sentiments in England during the Middle Ages*, 420–21.

6. Wright, *A History*, 437–38.

7. "God may send me a stripe or two," said one, "if my husband should see me here." "Nay," said Alice, another, "she that is afraid had better go home; I dread no man"; Wright, 438.

8. Wright, 439.

9. On the attack on the domineering wife, see D.E. Underdown, "The Taming of the Scold: The Enforcement of Patriarchal Authority in Early Modern England," in Order and Disorder in Early Modern England, eds. Anthony Fletcher and John Stevenson (Cambridge: University of Cambridge Press, 1986), 129.

10. Samuel K. Cohn, "Donne in piazza e donne in tribunale a Firenze nel rinascimento," in Studi Sorici 22, no. 3 (July–September 1981): 531–32.

11. See Underdown, "The Taming of the Scold," 116–36.

12. Bernard Capp, *When Gossips Meet: Women, Family, and Neighbourhood in Early Modern England* (Oxford: Oxford University Press, 2003), 117.

13. The literature on women's exclusion from crafts and guilds in England, as well as France, Germany, and Holland, is extensive. For England, see Alice Clark, *Working Life of Women in the Seventeenth Century* (London: Routledge & Kegan Paul, 1982 [1919]).

14. Marianne Hester, "Patriarchal Reconstruction and Witch Hunting," in *Witchcraft in Early Modern Europe: Studies in Culture and Belief*, eds. Jonathan Barry, Marianne Hester, and Gareth Roberts (Cambridge: Cambridge University Press, 1996), 302.

15. See, among others, Underdown, "The Taming of the Scold," 123.

16. Underdown, "The Taming of the Scold," 123–25; see also S.D. Amussen, "Gender, Family and the Social Order, 1560–1725," in Fletcher and Stevenson, Order and Disorder in Early Modern England, 215.

17. Underdown, "The Taming of the Scold," 123.

18. Louis B. Wright, *Middle-Class Culture in Elizabethan England* (Ithaca, NY: Cornell University Press, 1965 [1935]).

CHAPTER TWO

Formation

Waves of vapor
escaping
Lingering around
my lips always believing
Tongue in position.
Her wings
open
Searching for you
(all of us).
Song moves outside of herself
Joining others
       Singing, we fly

—carla bergman

Downstream Ritual

Lara Messersmith-Glavin

I am Lara, daughter of Stephanie, daughter of Evelyn, daughter of Frieda. These are the only names of my line that I know. I reach back into this lineage as if swimming a stream in the dark—I am borne on its waters and moved by its currents but unable to see its source. I am blind to the topographies, barriers, and weather that shaped it. In the stories of my family, in the narrative we build to tell us who we are and where we have come from, women are largely silent. Their names are first names, their histories absorbed into the flow of the men. Any women's wisdom from that line, any practices, have been lost to me.

"We are German" is the story I was given. My cultural inheritance is a deeply patriarchal family structure, a surname that sounds like a warplane, a love of fried potatoes, and a tendency to rage. Beyond that, my sense of having a people—an identity of roots in land and shared knowledge extending beyond my immediate families of origin and choice—is truncated and abstract.

My family's rituals consisted almost exclusively small, personal word games—playful rules about what to say when and why. At bedtime, we hugged and said, "Everything and lots of it," a shorthand for the lengthy verbal ritual I demanded as a small child. To this day, we call each other on the first of every month to blurt out, "Yeah, but! Yeah, but! Yeah but!" as many times as we can in one minute—we are forbidden to say the offending phrase any other time of the month. We have rhymes and sayings for arrivals, leave takings, and intolerable waits, but all these rituals reference our lives together in the manner of inside jokes. They tell nothing of where we came from before we were *us*.

Our big rituals were pedestrian and hollow—my parents taught me to celebrate Christian holidays, though as a Christian schoolmate once derided me, "You aren't Christians. You're rock 'n' rollers." At Christmas, my dad would watch football while my mom and I decorated a tree. Especially as an adolescent, I longed for the magic of candles and pine boughs, the spark of community that warms dark winter nights. Instead, my dad would say, "Christmas is for little kids," and shuffle off to the TV room. At Easter, they would hide candy and eggs around our yard, but we did not speak of springtime, growth, or rebirth. Going through these motions inspired more questions than answers: they transmitted no rich tradition or identity other than a white, middle-class, materialistic legacy that can be tracked through what's on sale in the seasonal section of any supermarket.

White people's narrative in North America is mostly a shameful exchange. Through colonialism and assimilation, we traded much of our historical knowledge and practices for power, and we are now reaping the rapid and bitter consequences of the dissolution of our ancestral ways of knowing. My story is of secular Christianity—of aggression and domination. We left our old ways behind long ago, and our new ways reflect different values, like impoverished relationships to land and community. The collective creation of meaning I participate in is largely commodified—small, weak tokens of ritual and passage: a prom dress, a driver's licence, a mortgage. Missing entirely is a shared sense of place and secret wisdom, mysteries lost through countless cycles of stealing from and eradicating other cultures and erasing women from history.

What does it mean for settlers to grow roots on stolen land? How long do we need to live in a place before we have deep ties to its land and movements? Is there another home to return to? How do we make a new home in our hearts, a place where our identities can grow together in community, and flow forward, into our children and others, carrying forward the best of what we have learned and rejecting the rest? My more immediate culture brought death to this continent and helped create a new culture wherein ritual, discipline, and meaning are available for purchase, and other ways of knowing are unvalued. It is this absence I have inherited.

Another thing I have inherited from my invisible ancestry is an auto-immune disease, which I developed immediately after giving birth to my child—a complex entry into motherhood. After my diagnosis, I was approached by a genetic-mapping company to help with their research on my chronic illness. I agreed, spat in the tube, and in exchange for my compliance, received a bewildering amount of information: a likely fear of heights, of smelling asparagus pee, of having early-onset Alzheimer's. But I also gained a brief glimpse past the narrative my family had bequeathed to me, an image of a history I didn't know I had. Ancestors—Celtic, Viking, Roma, Baltic, Ashkenazi—all obliterated by patrilineage that told our German story: its women lost in the flow, whispering to me from upstream.

I know I will never learn those women's private stories nor the choices and paths that led them into a line with a German name, but I now know they existed. One hundred, two hundred, five hundred years before me, there were women, from many places, whose names and secret practices I can never reclaim. But their memories, as traces, may yet sing in my blood. It feels significant to me that my body's transition into being a mother—a physical ritual of its own—triggered my disease and brought me closer to my lost lineage. My sense of history has folded in on itself, becoming richer, more convoluted, fuller of mystery and belonging.

At various points in my childhood, I imagined these alternate histories for myself. For reasons I could not explain, I made a menorah card at school in place of Christmas cards other first graders were making. My teacher was surprised but said, "Paulo and Lara don't celebrate Christmas. They celebrate Hanukkah. Would you like to tell us about this?" I let the other student do the talking—I had no details to give. I was sure Hanukkah was somehow important to me, even if my family had never said so, and honestly, I was not even sure what it was.

That evening, I asked my parents if we were Jewish. They laughed. "Not even a *little* bit?" I pleaded, panicking at the thought of the inappropriate card I had made. Not even a little bit, they assured me. And yet according to my genetic ancestry, my mother's line is indeed a little bit Jewish at one time, and a little bit Viking, and a little bit Roma, all cultures I felt drawn to at one time or another. How much of this was my imagination grasping at what was exotic to me in my white, rural town? How much was old memory, a deep urge tugging at the edges of my identity? To this day, I have no idea why I told the teacher what I did, but I suspect my six-year-old self was telling me something important about what she craved and needed.

My private childhood attempts at ritual were weird, messy things. We moved to eastern Oregon when I was seven and left behind the Midwestern smells of wet red clay, thunderstorms, and decaying corn fields. Our new home was in the high desert, flanked by ponderosas and stretches of low sage. I played at solitary magic, constructing amulets and altars from twigs and stones and finding flat places in rocks and on logs to arrange bits of stick, rubble, and woven pine. I skidded down the dry, loose-shale hillside between sere grasses, upsetting chittering grasshoppers and sending small rockslides clattering off ledges below. I plucked crunchy mosses from the jutting rocks and sought out cavelets in the shade where my esoteric tinkering felt safer and less susceptible to ridicule from the sun. This was not my place, and I knew it. No part of that land held a familiar voice for me—it lived and was full of stories, that much was clear but its stories were not mine, and nor did my family have the language to hear them or follow them into a deeper understanding of the land. We were outsiders in that crisp, amber world. In the absence of roots, I often felt dizzy and incomplete, pushed away from the earth, as if polarized by a magnetic field.

My favourite place was on the water in Alaska, where we lived and worked in the summer as fishermen. I felt at home near the horror of vast waves; the sigh, calm, and crash of breakers against sand and stone; the damp; the fog snagging on outcroppings; and the seep and rivulet of springs. My sand altars on the beach were intuitive and beautiful. My seaweed weavings were sure. All I had to do was line shells up on a jut of driftwood to feel like I had unlocked some arcane tessellation or revealed a secret chord. Beyond patterns and reason, there was a sense of great potential and purpose that rang in these moments, when it felt like panes of glass aligned and I could see through the world to many layers beyond. I did not know what it meant, but it assured me things *had meaning.*

As I moved into adolescence, I began chasing that meaning more intently. The messages I received at home were confusing—an atheist on the one hand, an agnostic on the other, each offering duelling takes on god. But more than god, I craved ritual and sought it out through institutions that felt like acceptable compromises. At thirteen, I tried the Episcopal church, which admitted gay people and had a woman minister. Her voice was deep and soothing, and I loved the trappings of the service: the candles and incense, the anointing oil and water from the River Jordan, the darkness and light, the chanting, the communion. It felt superficially comforting but ultimately empty, a corrective, punitive feeling to the service standing between myself and wholeness.

A girlfriend and I, when we were fifteen, sought ritual in strangeness—we removed our clothes in exchange for capes, we smeared one another with pudding as if it were mud, we cut our wrists and thighs with hunting knives and daubed stones on one another's faces with blood, and we held antlers to our brows, feeling a deep, unclear urge. We giggled and swooned through these movements, re-enacting something spontaneous and remembered, but we lacked the guidance to give it the formal weight of tradition or witness.

What impulse guided us? What instinct shaped our movements and symbols? Looking back, I think we pulled meaning from the past, reaching for intuitive senses of who we were and for cultural forms that may have shaped those who came before us. It was as if a great river of symbols and practices carved a path long before us but had since run dry, diverted to this channel or that, dried up from drought and endless wheels of summer. Only the faintest trickle moved through us, little more than a silly urge. We were play acting with the solemn drama of adolescence, and yet it was there—a longing for something long lost.

Do we carry the memory of meaning-making within us? Does it still live in our bodies, dormant but restless, triggered at times by this song or that scent or a dream we cannot place upon waking? The egg each of us was formed from was intact in our biological mothers when they were inside their mothers. This can transmit feelings, traumas, tendencies, and perhaps even encoded memories across generations. In this sense, we are not individuals: we are temporary manifestations of a flow of effects embedded in dynamic circumstances. Do we have a way back to the ancestral knowledge we lost?

As I grew older, I learned to place my longing historically. I recognize my experiences as a patriarchal separation from place and practice. I see how the stories and histories I learned prioritize types of obedience and how they control our collective narratives. The erasures and angles are clear. I know now, too, that I am the beneficiary of countless longings, heartaches, wonders, beliefs, and moments of courage, all humming through my genetic code. My loss is not abstract. There were real women, and they lived in this place and that: Ireland, the coast of Sweden, Romania. I have slowly begun rebuilding a sense of old tradition—reading and learning the bits of their lives I can glean from history books and from listening to those who came before me. I learn their myths, their battles with conquerors and new religions, and their assimilations into this nation and that.

The old religions teem with characters I examine for familiarity or a sense of truth: the Oak King, the Holly King, Rán and Aegir, and Thor and Odin. I sink into these stories, looking not just for symbols and frames to make sense of the world but also very specifically for practices that will help me and my community mark time and significance, celebrate together, with a sense of continuity and meaning, so that we may participate in our own histories without also taking what is not ours. And yet, going through these motions, aping old rituals and talking to gods who never lived where I now walk, also tells me that these are not aspects of my culture, either.

My alienation and fractured self are my cultural inheritance. Sometimes I feel like I am stranded in the present, and no amount of recollection will return to me the authenticity and wholeness I crave. I cannot summon old spirits and memories in the here and now. Once that line of transmission is broken, my attempts to recreate it on my own feel hollow. Ritual is about capturing tradition and answering questions—providing focus, form, and witness to things we find collectively important. It is also about locating our small selves in a much longer stream of aesthetics and belief, even as the rituals themselves slowly evolve over time. Where does continuity end and creation begin?

My child is six. They love superheroes, science, ninjas, and myths. In winter, we trim holly from the bush in our back yard and drape it throughout our home. We decorate a tree. We burn things on solstice and talk about the Oak King coming back with the light. We trade gifts on Christmas, which has everything to do with the story of Santa and nothing to do with Christ. In spring, we cheer on the appearance of small buds and colour boiled eggs. In midsummer, we tell stories of the Holly King's return. My child believes in fairies but not a god. They know some Christians, Muslims, Jews, and Buddhists but mostly witches, a word they struggle to reconcile with the green-faced cacklers of drugstore Halloween.

I watch them swim through this incoherent soup of symbols, marvelling at how these symbols, once meaningful and stable, have become disorienting and contradictory in our contemporary world. My child seems fine with it now, cleaving to scientific explanations while enjoying mythology's wonders and monsters. They ask a different question every night at bedtime—"Mama, how do they make reflection and shadow? How do they make matter?"—as if the fundamental tools of physics were cobbled together in a workshop by powerful cosmic elves.

Their curiosity about the origins of things leads them onto the strange terrain where science and myth sound the same—the Big Bang, the inability to create or destroy matter or energy, the role of genetics and evolution. Yet, someday they will have questions about their family origins. They may feel hollowness in their heart where ritual should live. How do I help them find the shapes that will best fill that space? We are not Celts. We are not Jewish. We are something else, something new and strange on occupied land—yet land we also know and love as best we know how.

When the beautiful walnut tree in front of our house died, we wept together. Before it was taken down, we called our neighbors to stand with us: to watch the squirrels scamper through its brittle branches, to explain to the crows what was about to happen, and to tell stories about times we'd spent beneath its leaves. My child tied a cord around its trunk, tucking into the knot small twigs and flowers from around our yard. They cut a length of the same cord and tied it about each of our wrists. "A connection bracelet," they said. They hugged the tree and thanked it for its place in our lives. We felt good and whole, which eased the pain of losing the tree, and it helped us mark the transition in a way that felt honorable. With that ritual, my child learned we can make meaning in our own ways: that we can decide what is important, and that we have people around us who will stand witness as we mark the passage of time.

Spirit. Magic. Revolution.

Shaunga Tagore

He's not in there.

The shape of his nose is different.

That must have happened while they were embalming him. Thank you for this information, years of watching Six Feet Under.

This was my inner dialogue while looking at him for the first time ever, without his soul in his body.

Dressing his body with pink and white roses.

Playing the piano for him.

Listening to my mother sing.

Reciting the children's Last Rites.

Wearing my birthday dress.

My mother's voice: *"It is your job to press the button to start the fire on the cremation machine. I cannot do it. It is the children's last sacred duty."*

Deep breath. I ask my Higher Self to tell me what ritual to catalyze, what healing to release, what words the Universe can give me, to honour these three buttons?

Spirit.

Magic.

Revolution.

I am here today to talk about forgiveness.

Wait.

Before I go on, let me repeat that so you can pay attention to how your body reacts when I say it.

Forgiveness.

What I immediately feel is defensiveness. I bristle and I turn brittle. My insides morph into armour. My body rejects the word.

And what a loaded word! In break-ups, situations of abuse, interpersonal conflicts, and all sorts of relationship deaths, many people say you need to be able to *forgive* in order to move on.

Others react exactly the way my body did. They say you don't owe anyone your forgiveness, especially not if they've abused or harmed you.

Some people will clarify: this is about the importance of *forgiving yourself.* Forgive yourself for *staying too long,* for not doing the *right* thing, for all the burdens you carry.

Others complicate even further: if your inability to forgive someone is hindering your ability to be free, then yes, forgive them. But do it for yourself.

I get why we react to the word. The language of forgiveness has been so often used as a tool for gaslighting, dismissing and minimizing violence; as an accountability cop-out, an excuse to evade responsibility, and an emotional manipulation tactic to get others to comfort you, or feel sorry for you, when you're the one who did the harm.

Please forgive me . . .

. . . is someone apologizing for how bad they feel without ever apologizing for what they've done. Promising they'll never do it again without challenging or even knowing why they did it in the first place.

This applies on a collective level too, say when it comes to racism within feminist and queer liberation movements. So often, the pain of Black, Indigenous and people of colour (BIPOC) is eclipsed by white people's shame in coming to terms with their part in history and current reality. In these instances, white people need BIPOC folks to *forgive* them for their racism before they feel able to take action as allies. *Please absolve me of my guilt, otherwise I am stuck in my pain and cannot move out or through.*

Please forgive me is a way to ensure a false sense of intimacy and care so that both the relationship and the dynamic of abuse can stay intact. In other words, forgiveness is used as a tool to ensure that things do not change. *Please forgive me so that I can continue to deny and evade the problem, so that I, personally, do not have to change.*

As individuals and communities, we are terrified of what we would have to lose—and feel—if we did, indeed, change.

The truth is, in order to heal, we must be willing to lose.

Like you know when you're writing a story, and you know it's not working, and your editor comes to you and says, "This is great! Everything will come together, you just have to get rid of this one part."

And you're like, "Noooo! That's my favourite part!"

Sometimes we have to get rid of our favourite part in order for our story to work.

What if the Universe sat you down in your living room and said, "Listen, everything in your life will come together; you just have to let go of this one thing. I know you're really attached to it, but it's the *one thing* holding you back."

The truth is, real love does not come without loss. If we want to be open to loving each other better, we also must be open to losing our attachment to control. Our belief that we can somehow avoid getting hurt. Our walls we enclose around our vulnerability. Our emotional and spiritual habits that keep us stuck in cycles of doing harm and being harmed.

Loving someone endlessly means knowing we won't stop loving them after their body is finished. If they go before we go, we'll have to live with that pain.

If we want to win big in our lives and as people who care about a collectively liberated world, we need to be okay with losing just as big.

Here's the twist: I don't believe this happens without genuine forgiveness. Life has taught me a more authentic definition of the word. Forgiveness *as an honest and complete acceptance of reality.*

What if forgiveness is choosing to not abandon yourself? What if it means learning to be present with yourself long enough to understand how you were harmed, and how you caused harm? Being curious about your choices and why you made them. Wholly accepting the reality of the situation and how you participated in it. Forgiveness is space. It is silence. It isn't attached to any one outcome. Where you don't need anyone to hold your hand or make you feel better. Forgiveness isn't given or received, it's just there because you own it.

Forgiveness, the complete and honest acceptance of yourself, exactly as you are. And in that silence, what speaks is *hope*.

That, yes, I am willing and able to change.

Before my father passed away, in his hospital bed, he asked me if I was mad at him.

Without planning it, I heard myself say:

"No, not at all. All is forgiven."

The raincloud in his body gently lifted into the air, dissipating. In its place was an orange and yellow glow, the rising sun.

"Yes," he replied. "It is best to leave without any burdens."

It was a while before I realized this was the last conversation we had. He left a week later. He was in so much pain, he only spoke when absolutely necessary. And we had said everything we needed to say.

In this silence, I felt every hard time we ever experienced together lift away, so easily. In this silence, I heard the cleansing rivers of the planet moving through us, louder and louder.

In this silence, the most powerful agent of transformation.

Death. Fire. Rebirth.

Spirit.

Magic.

Revolution.

The Scrutiny of Now

Maneo Mohale

Dumelang. Lebitso laka ke Maneo Refiloe Mohale. Mme waka ke Susan Mohale, ntate waka ke Bonang Francis Mohale, ausi waka ke Tshepiso Serialong Mohale. Ke ngoanyana wa Mosotho, ke bua Sesotho, ke Mokoena waha Mokotedi, ke mokgodutswane o moholo, o jarile lehlabathe ka moko- kotlo, ke leruarua la moradi wa Mohale, ea sesa 'Koena...Ke leboha batho ba Coast Salish, ke leboha batho ba Musqueam, ka mehla.

My name is Maneo Refiloe Mohale. I am a Mosotho from Johannesburg, South Africa. I wanted to first address you with my mother tongue, Sesotho, and by introducing my family's clan and totem: the crocodile.

In Sesotho, we greet each other by saying "Dumela," if speaking to one person, or "Dumelang," if speaking to many people. *Dumela* means "yes," or to agree or consent. The way we usually reply is by saying the same or "Ashe," to which the greeter then asks "O kae?" which functions as "How are you?" but literally means "Where are you?"

The story goes that in the time before time as we know it—or the time before colonial time—we needed each other to agree about *being* a human and not, as my father puts it, a creature in the bush trying to eat you. In the event that my ancestors were in the open and heard someone approaching, they could cry "Dumela," or "Agree that you are a person!" to which the person approaching would reply "Ashe!" or "Yes!" The natural response after what I would imagine would be a sigh of relief would be "O kae?" or "Where are you?" They would each, then, embrace the other as only they could, without fear, knowing and recognizing each other as people.

. Much of my work—as a scholar, writer, and activist—centres both these principles of personhood and the recognition, or honouring, of shared humanity at its centre, either consciously or unconsciously.

OF BLUES AND BEAUTY

A couple years ago, as part of my job at the time, at the South African non-profit organization Auwal Socio-Economic Research Institute, I was privileged to listen to my father's speech in front of a remarkably brilliant and diverse group of fellows I worked with every day. My team had invited him to speak on leadership, and it was pleasantly mortifying to sit and listen to my dad speak in his usual gracious and passionate way—sort of like Bring Your Parent to Work Day.

In his talk, my father explained "The Tyranny of the OR and the Genius of the AND" from one of his favourite books, *Built to Last*, by two American business experts, James Collins and Jerry Porras. Though I had heard my father speak of this idea before—the power of rejecting binary oppositions (OR's tyranny) and learning to hold two seemingly conflicting ideas at once (AND's genius)—something about hearing these from my father's mouth this time sparked something in me.

So in my growing desire to extend my own Black—feminist—womanist praxis, I could not resist the delicious opportunity to insert my own voice into the archive while, possibly, subverting the ideas of white men. Thus, this piece is titled "The Scrutiny of Now" (I'll get to that in a bit). I want to unpack "tyranny" and "genius" and reassemble them in ways that make sense to me. So, instead of "The Tyranny of the OR," and "The Genius of the AND," I propose "The Blues of the OR, and the Beauty of the AND."

I will use these two ideas to talk about aspects dear to me: Blackness, queerness, and the complexities of carving out our own spaces where, in our own communities, we can recognize and affirm each other's humanity. I will use these two ideas, The Blues of the OR, and the Beauty of the AND, to talk about solidarity and porousness, dissolution, and ever-shifting membranes between Self and Other—as well as relationships between both speech and silence and past and present. I will do this through my own understandings, lessons I was lucky to learn, moments I was witness to, and my ever-expanding experiences.

THE BLUES

Sometime ago, while I was still living on Turtle Island, I had the mind-blowing honour of listening to and meeting Professor Patricia Hill Collins, a brilliant and massively influential Black feminist writer, sociologist, and educator. In her public lecture, she spoke about the blues in ways that pushed the blues beyond genre and even art form. She revealed the blues as an unmistakeably Black distillation of centuries of oppression, slavery, ancestry, migration, and endless labour, saturated and redolent with the tensions between loneliness and belonging.

What better vessel than the blues to talk about my relationship to complex and dissonant ideas of race, gender, and sexuality in non-fixed, non-binary, non-tyrannical ways? The blues is rooted in liminal spaces like Congo Square in New Orleans, where African slaves, taken from the continent of my birth, mixed the songs they carried on their tongues with the strange new air in New Orleans, interrupting space with embodied song and memory.

A genre where, in the 1920s, Black women like Ma Rainey and Bessie Smith howled their night songs about the dangerous, dark art of loving other women—their queerness oozing from thick and sultry lyrics of their songs. In her poem "Just how some folks play the blues," Jillian Christmas, the gorgeous slam poetry champion and former codirector of the Verses Festival of Words, calls Bessie Smith and Ma Rainey:

> Two BLACK renaissance women, friends,
>   singing about the thing that would have them jailed again and again.
> Both of them, with their men,
>   it didn't matter, they couldn't keep that song off of their lips.

In a similar way, I also cannot keep *my* song off my lips. Whether of my people's history, unspeakable joy and unspeakable violence, dispossession, or apartheid and now post-apartheid apartheid, my song radiates and ripples from the colour of my skin. I have another song, too—less obvious and quieter, a song of my desire, attraction, connection, and love of people (no matter where they fall on the gender spectrum), a song I sometimes call queer. I cannot help but keep these songs on my lips, even if I, more often than not, feel as if I am holding contradictory chords, uncomfortable and dissonant, in my mouth.

This is the blues of the "OR," and it makes space for dissonance, which marks it as beautiful.

In the effort of talking things through, being heard, and finally coming to the theme of my piece, "The Scrutiny of Now," I include a piece, below, that I wrote for an amazing platform called *HOLAA! (HOLAA!* is a pan-African, queer womanist collective that is home to my writing, helmed by folks like Tiffany Kagure Mugo, and features fierce queer and trans Black African thinkers like HeJin Kim, Wanelisa Xaba and Sibongile Shope.)

#FORBLACKGIRLSONLY AND THE GLORIOUS UNEASINESS OF SISTERHOOD

I have this T-shirt. It is simple, black, and fits me snugly like a hug from an old friend you have not seen in some time. Across the front, in large, bold, white letters is a phrase, powerful in its simplicity and maybe a little cheeky, audacious even: "Black, Queer, and unapologetic." It is the kind of T-shirt I have always wanted to own, and when I eagerly snapped it up at a poetry event, I fantasized about all the spaces where I could flaunt it—my obviously political fashion statement. I imagined the conversations it would spark at home, the curious whispers at my back as I wore these facets of my identity, so visibly, with pride and on my own terms.

I tried to imagine my mother's face. Would she be able to find and recognize me somewhere within the white printed words on my chest? Or in the black spaces between them? Would she lower her eyes if I entered our kitchen at home with that T-shirt over a pair of blue jeans? Could I wear it without apology there?

Despite my initial excitement, the T-shirt spent more time neatly folded in the dark corners of my cupboard than it did being worn fearlessly in the open Johannesburg air. I had mostly given up wearing it in public until I heard of the #ForBlackGirlsOnly picnic in Cape Town. The picnic was to be organized by BlackLoveSessions, a South African group that powerfully described itself on its Facebook page as "a radical social movement unapologetically promoting Blackness around Cape Town through a series of events, talks, and exhibitions." Reading this, my eyes fixated on the word *unapologetically*. I immediately knew two things: I would fly, without hesitation, to Cape Town to attend and I would wear that T-shirt.

Stepping off the plane, I left my luggage at a trendy boutique hotel in Cape Town's city bowl and changed, switching out the colourful printed T-shirt I was wearing for my appropriately political T-shirt. Quickly catching a branded taxi to the picnic, I felt fake. I was a young, queer, Black, middle-class girl who could afford a flight at a moment's notice and to stay in upscale comfort in Cape Town, a city notorious for unapologetic whiteness and its disgust, pity, and shame for Black life. I felt complicit in the city's whiteness and in its project to either assimilate or marginalise Blackness, in its effort to ultimately erase Black people and our supposed unsightliness. I felt like a white sheep in revolutionary clothing, the much-discussed and debated coconut.

Upon arrival, I entered the bar where the picnic was to be held, but I did so tentatively, as an imposter would—slowly and ready to be exposed. What I saw when I reached the bar's grassy backyard genuinely shook me. In front of me were hundreds of Black women, brazenly dressed in black: sitting, standing, dancing, drinking, eating, selling products, tweeting, photographing, writing, documenting, meeting each other, and laughing. I stood, moved in ways I honestly find difficult to describe, with a kind of relief and absurd joy, but also a kind of fleeting grief and an aching realization that I had never been surrounded by so many Black girls simply *being* in one space: gorgeously, improbably, astonishingly.

From that moment on, I spent the day in a space that pivoted between an overwhelming sense of belonging and support and a fragile, tense sense of sisterhood. There were moments of fist-pumping, *yaaaasssss*-inspiring recognition. I shout-sang Erykah Badu's "Tyrone" with shrill and gorgeous abandon alongside hundreds of other voices. I danced to Thandiswa Mazwai's "Ingoma," with no one to gape at my thighs or police my twerk.

I sat in uneasy gratitude as panellists and fellow black-clad women called out the transphobia, ableism, classism, and homophobia far too often overlooked in spaces that proclaim surface "sisterhood" without a thorough acknowledgement and analysis of how our privileges and oppressions work to include certain bodies and exclude others.

The most challenging and perhaps the most important moments for me, though, were intense disagreements about issues exposing the barriers between us as Black women—our competing and conflicting experiences, desires, and visions of Black womanhood. These difficult, precious moments glimpsed how we could build upon our urgent, ever-deepening desire to be free, both in how we are and where we are.

Before I left the miraculous and unforgettable picnic, I was overwhelmed with gratitude, complex feelings of contradiction and comfort, with thoughts of the myriad ways in which Black women experience violence and feel pain while hurting each other, and hopeful imaginings of how I could immerse myself in the "hard work and scrutiny of now."

SELF OR OTHERS; SELF AND OTHERS

Since that Cape Town picnic, and after moving to my home city, Johannesburg, we at #ForBlackGirlsOnly had another event, a much larger one with a greater impact on South African public discourse. I was fortunate to emcee the event and organize alongside many amazing Black queer women I am fortunate to know and look up to. In many ways, #ForBlackGirlsOnly has become my political home, one with plenty of room for complexities, contradictions, and tensions—both blues and beauty.

And yet, many people did not understand our need for a spaces like the ones #ForBlackGirlsOnly created. The vitriol, hatred, accusations of "reverse racism," and threats of intense violence were frequent in the event's run-up. Organizers had to fundraise for barricades and security personnel at the event location, Constitution Hill. Radio, Twitter, Facebook, and talk shows were abuzz about whether a space like this was "divisive" or "destructive" to the ever-crumbling edifice of "The Rainbow Nation." I remember scrolling through rape threats (particularly threats of sexual violence that are reserved exclusively for Black queer women—the supposedly "curative" kind), comments appealing to national unity at the expense of Black lives, to the tune of: "If we complain that white people did this in the past and continue to do this, what will white people think of us now?"

This broke my heart: there was and is little ambiguity in how whiteness perceives Blackness inside a society that is still representative of a deeply violent (and global) white supremacist system. True solidarity or unity, I feel, should not come at the expense of another's humanity.

Ultimately, #ForBlackGirlsOnly was very deliberately not about whiteness. It was about providing a space where racialized transgender and cisgender women and non-binary people could gather safely in a shared space, with possibilities for healing love, sharing, and grace with people who perhaps shared in their unique experiences of moving through the world, if only briefly.

Even before then, the work of justifying our right to exist and gather was unbelievably exhausting and demoralizing. And in trying to draw strength and validation from my loves, I looked to examples around me: groups such as No One Is Illegal and #BlackLivesMatter give me immense hope—they incorporate both the blues and beauty of the "OR" and "AND," self and community, and me and you.

I remembered that whether it was studying my Honours in History at the University of British Columbia, or my involvement in various organisations and movements alongside incredible people within campus activism (with the Sexual Assault Support Centre or the March to Reclaim Consent), online activism (*The Talon*), or community activism (the Purple Thistle art and activism centre and #ForBlackGirlsOnly), I have gravitated to movements and efforts that centre marginalized people's humanity (which is so often overlooked, threatened, disrespected or denied) at their centres, and the human rights they are imbued with.

I am infinitely grateful to the people who have marched, sung, slammed, raged, cried, and created with me; who have held space for my mistakes and fear; and who teach me in myriad ways.

This is an excerpt from a talk given at EMMA Talks, Vancouver, BC. The full talk is here: http://emmatalks.org/video/maneo-mohale/

All the Ways that Capitalism Sucks (or at Least Some of Them)

Kian Cham

When I wrote my EMMA Talk in April 2015, I was a youth at the Purple Thistle and went by my birth name, Kelsey, which means "fierce island" in Old Norse and "warrior" in Irish Gaelic. Having chosen to medically transition, I have since given myself the name Kian, which means "ancient" or "enduring" in Irish Gaelic. For me, these names signify timeless, enduring struggle, and resilience in the regenerative ancestral, cultural, and spiritual relationships I share with those on homelands I have yet to visit and with those on lands I am connected to as an uninvited guest. My EMMA Talk offers insight and continues to inform where I am in my life now.

Growing up, I was a cute kid, but then all kids are pretty cute. I liked Batman, reading R.L. Stein books, martial arts, and competing with my sister, who is four years older than me. I grew up in Surrey, BC, which is the territory of the Katzie, Semyome, Kwantlen, and Tsawwassen Peoples, but I did not learn that until much later in life. I played with my neighbourhood friends a lot—Lava Tag, basketball, forts in the blackberry bushes where adults wouldn't find us, bike races, barely tied roller blades, water guns, cherry pit fights, adventures in the forest, and N64 Mario games. I had a pretty awesome suburban childhood, with great parents and a funny crew of neighborhood kids to grow up with. Besides some weird, subtly racist stuff in school—like people making fun of the *mahu* sandwiches my mom made for me, which led me to hide the food I loved in my desk until it got mouldy—and being called names like *Chinky*, life was pretty good. I was free to explore with my friends and dress how I wanted, which was lucky because I wanted to dress like a stylish nineties dude. And then I hit Grade 7 and puberty.

Until then, I was pretty much always seen as a boy. I was stoked about this, considering my favourite song growing up was "I'm a Boy" by the Who. But when I hit puberty, kids knew something was up. No matter how I hunched or how baggy my shirts were, douchebag kids said awful stuff to me and would sometimes pick fights. I remember I really liked this one girl at summer golf lessons in Grade 7. She was awesome and I had hoped she saw me for me. At the end of camp, which was probably two weeks, we had a big tournament and were matched in groups of four—me, this girl, and two annoying dudes. During the entire game they made fun of me, asking why I dressed like a boy. I was pissed, not so much because they were harassing me but because they had outed me to this girl. I thought, damn, now she knows I am a girl and will never like me. By the end of summer, I knew I needed a solution: I could either start high school and be ostracized by ding-dongs calling me *dyke*, a word I did not relate to since I was really a boy, or conform. I decided I would try to protect my physical self by sacrificing my personal identity. So, with some struggle, I learned to be a girl.

Over a couple years, some pretty great friends taught me female swagger. I grew my hair super long, started wearing eyeliner, and plucked my eyebrows. A friend said I went from being a caterpillar to a butterfly. The problem was I still felt like an imposter, and I feared being caught out. I was pissed—things did not feel right. The world felt like a lie. It felt ridiculous. I had to be this other person just to not get my ass kicked; it was just like when kids in my class were made fun of for eating Jell-O out of Tupperware containers. I felt shitty because people made fun of other kids for being on welfare, for being Jews and Hindus, or for being dykes and faggots, especially since most of the time those accusations were not even true—and even if they were, so what? It is shitty that all those names and words were social bombs people dropped, not words representing stories and experiences we respected.

Why do we use names to shame one another? Mostly so those dropping the bombs can stay afloat. I recognized these patterns and connected them to stories I read in newspapers every day. I did my best not to connect them to my personal life, though I know the addiction to hard drugs and partying I soon developed was hella related to how I had to learn to be a girl to survive high school. In any case, that was the time of my life when I wrote a lot of angry poetry.

Later, after I turned eighteen, I left Surrey for Montreal, where I met my first gender-bending friends and learned to be myself. People in Montreal were more accepting than in Surrey. When I cut my hair off, I recognized myself in the mirror. That was a pretty neat moment. I still had a bunch of crap to deal with, though—stuff doesn't work out magically in an instant. During my first year in Montreal, before I cut my hair, I was attracting assholes who thought I looked exotic and challenging to date. I ended up dating a few emotionally abusive dudes who messed me up. That led to a lot of mistrust. At the time, I had been training in karate for nationals—I was trying to get away from the drug scene this way, so I was often at the gym trying a lot to meet my coaches' expectations. This guy I was dating would come to my work and bring me lunches—poutine and burgers. I thought that was pretty nice. Then I noticed I was gaining quite a lot of weight for my size and started feeling insecure, which was hard since doing drugs had kept me skinny before. Having been socialized as a girl, it was hard not being so-called perfect and small—when I presented feminine, people constantly commented on my body.

After this guy and I broke up, he told me he had been feeding me junk because he saw I was gaining muscle and that turned him off. He had been bringing me food to make me gain fat. It is a psychological *fuck you* when someone manipulates your body to suit their messed-up ideas. I dated many shittier people in my late teens and early twenties—and there are many more men doing messed-up stuff to many women right now. After I cut my hair off, shitty dudes like that one stopped wanting to date me. It is unfortunate this is what it took for me to prevent those interactions.

Unfortunately, living in the masculine world brought attention by dudes who recognized I was born female. I have been stopped numerous times—either by myself or by friends—from getting into fights with ignorant homophobes and transphobes. I have been called a dyke while walking down the street, and I have had my head smashed into a brick wall by a bunch of young white guys who shouted, "Are you a boy or are you a girl?" I had witnessed them beating on a young Indigenous woman, and I was scared for her life, so I interfered. In any case, after that episode, walking down the street and riding the bus in Montreal was too triggering—every group of white dudes in fitted Armani-type shirts freaked me out. So when a person I cared for was about to move to Vancouver, I chose to follow that romance. It brought me closer to my family, and it is where I found community support.

When I got to BC, I started doing two things: karate, with my long-time friend Sota, whom I had been practising with since I was ten, and gardening, with a youth-run collective, the Purple Thistle Centre in East Vancouver. These things affected my life in more ways than I can imagine.

I learned a lot more at the Purple Thistle than how to garden, which I was interested in to counter and resist corporate systems of greed in the world. The Purple Thistle is collectively organized by participants, which means there is no hierarchy. There are no bosses, no youth workers, and no leaders. No one tells us what to do. When I came to the Thistle, I had never experienced that. Even though I was totally new and nobody knew me, people trusted me with responsibility from my first day. Nobody watched over me. People told me I could do as little or as much as I wanted. Because we were all just figuring stuff out, it was totally fine if things didn't work out. We could make mistakes. Projects could fail. It was all part of the learning process. This was huge for me since I am a person who will not do things I am not good at.

At the Thistle, I learned a ton from people of all types. I learned about compost and compost tea, fruit trees and plants that work together, plants that attract pollinating insects (like bees and butterflies), and fungus that connects to the roots of plants and feeds them water and nutrients. I got into medicinal plants, soil life, and the list goes on and continues to go on.

During my first year gardening with the Purple Thistle, our collective made a point of learning about the land we were working on, which is around the industrial wasteland of Vernon and Charles streets, right next to Clark Drive and right around all the scrap-metal yards and train tracks. We learned that the land beneath the hot, loud, concrete jungle inhabited by trucks and illegal garbage dumps had originally been a wet bog home to many animals, like elk, I could never see in the city. That was before 1910, when the City of Vancouver paid CN to fill the bog with part of Burnaby Mountain—and likely with garbage, too. I learned Captain Stamp, a hundred and fifty years after the settlers arrived, had put up Vancouver's first sawmill and that it only took one generation to destroy the ancient Douglas fir rainforest and replaced it with an early version of Vancouver's industrial downtown. Coast Salish Peoples and animals were displaced for the benefit of the capitalist economy, and settlers who participated in that system moved into new industrialized homes on unceded land they stole.

Learning this changed my outlook in life: it was the first time the history of settlers and Indigenous Peoples was presented to me straight up. White people came here to profit from and exploit the land, and to do so, they had to get through the hereditary caregivers of that land. In any case, our youth collective decided we wanted to learn how to garden and how our gardens came to be.

I was also studying a different kind of karate practice than before. From ages ten to twenty, I had been training in competitive sport karate. My new karate practice was based on traditional Japanese principles of *ki*, an internal energy that comes from finding harmony in your body and the external world. Having grown up in an America-dominated culture that prioritizes isolated muscle building, many concepts I was learning in karate conflicted directly with what I knew growing up. I was learning the body has its own invisible power that we in Western culture learn to shut off through isolation and entitlement. This karate taught me to find connection so power can flow again. It is rooted in an experiential understanding that our bodies are intuitive and can protect us quicker than our brains (if we can ever get over our brains and how big they are). For example, if I am biking, a bug might fly toward my eyeball, but right before it does, my eyelids blink shut. My brain does not notice until after. It takes half a second for the brain to process the bug, but our bodies are faster and can react to protect us—if only we can connect to them again. Interestingly, I have a tough time accepting this kind of karate into my life in a committed way. And I have a feeling I'm not totally ready to accept the truths of it, because to do so would mean accepting the stories of deception too.

For the past few years, I have been trying to listen to more stories and to learn the protocols of the land and peoples where my family chose to settle—so-called British Columbia, Canada. This is a hard and complicated process because the stories of this land are often filled with historical and ongoing trauma caused by all levels of government: colonially imposed First Nations' governments and Band Councils and big-time industry that settlers and many Indigenous Peoples have come to depend on for their livelihoods. We are in a sick system that perpetuates sickness.

Despite this sick system, people are choosing to live alternatively. This past weekend my partner and I visited friends in St'at'imc Nation. There in the mountains of the Yalakom Valley, our friends have established a new reoccupation camp. We listened to the experiences of two Indigenous women, spiritual warriors to reconnect to their culture and Traditional Practices and to stop dirty logging in their backcountry. We made food together over the fire, ate in a circle, and listened to one another's stories. They told us about the mountain cold at night and how they found tricks to use the fire to stay warm while they kept safe from sparks. We learned more about the camp's Protocol and how it is being led and directed by Xwisten Elders of that Territory.

Our friends told us about their Territory's history since settler colonization. We learned where their parents went to residential school and how settlers they trusted tore up their plant patches with lawn mowers after learning of those plants' medicinal values. I learned about Indian agents and how Indigenous Peoples in Canada had been unable to practise their cultural Ceremonies and speak their languages and how their children had been taken from their homes and brought to abusive residential schools. It was a heavy weekend—but also a really nurturing one. I had become sick the night before going to the mountain, but once there, I received more cold and flu remedies than I ever had before—so much love, care, knowledge and openness. There are good people in the world, and I'm honoured to have some in my life.

The ocean is warming and becoming more acidic. Climate change is causing super storms and forcing Indigenous peoples all over the world, from Haiti to the Philippines, into extreme poverty. People in this dominant culture are shutting down and numbing—they are doing drugs, playing video games obsessively, Facebooking, playing the stock market, gambling, and overworking. Capitalism is destroying us—individually, culturally, familially, nationally, environmentally, etc. Because of the economic system social pressure to be financially successful, the law, lack of fluidity in the educational system, and addictions, my immediate family has felt disconnected and is fighting hard to keep it together. This is not easy, but it is courageous, and I admire my parents for their determination to keep us connected, together, and supportive of each other.

So, this is where I talk about solidarity. It took me a long time of being part of activist circles before I understood what solidarity meant. To me, it means community action that supports struggle. This can look like a lot of things for a lot of people. Stopping the RCMP from displacing a blockade is one form of support that many people just cannot do right now. Donating money to causes you believe in, informing yourself, and talking to your friends and family about what you are learning is another form. Writing grants, sharing Internet resources, and using social media are other supportive actions. Making art and music to tell stories are, too. We can be creative in how we stand in solidarity. The more we do this, the more we recognize that changing Western culture will take all of us. By interconnecting our struggles, we connect our lessons and build community resiliency. We gain creative freedom if our work is founded on real relationships and we extend ourselves outwardly. We help these relationships grow stronger by building foundations of trust, joy, and compassion. With these relationships, we can affect change beyond ourselves and create inspired communities of support that defy the violent systems we live in.

The amazing people at the Purple Thistle did this for fifteen years, and it is what is happening at the Voice of the Voiceless Camp, the Unist'ot'en Camp, the Madii Lii Camp, and the Gitmundem Camp. It is what Ancestral Pride does and the Secwepemc Women's Warrior Society and Wolverine, the eighty-four-year-old Secwepemc man who tended an eight-acre garden by himself to feed his community's Elders, families, and frontline land defenders. It is also what my mom and dad do by keeping our family together. And encouraged us to act on what we believe in this messed-up world. Even though my mom says she does not have the courage to stand up and talk to an audience, she has deeper courage that is reflected in how she stands up every day to her responsibilities, with the people in her work life, with her friends and family, and by sacrificing her time and freedom. She is a role model, like many others, because she has the courage to defend and support what she loves.

....

This is an adaptation and update of the EMMA Talk delivered on April 6, 2015, in Vancouver, BC: http://emmatalks.org/video/kelsey-cham-corbett/

Being Democratic

Dorothy Woodend

When I thought about what I wanted to include in this anthology, I took a look at some of my recent work. As a film critic, I deal with the temporal. Films come and go, stuff moves quickly, and there are always new releases and the next big thing. What I find fascinating about Astra Taylor's films is that they wrestle with ideas that have stumped humans for millennia. How do you build a better society? What does democracy really mean? and What the heck is it all about? Her work is alive with the spirit of genuine inquiry—searching, talking, and sometimes failing to find answers but always asking the fundamental question of what it means to be human.

Astra Taylor's documentary *What is Democracy?* starts with a question and then adds another and then another until there is a teetering pile of queries, such as, Can democracy ever live up to its promise? What does it mean to have a happy life? Do people want to rule themselves? Is democracy worth fighting for?

And running underneath it all, that old Socratic question: How shall we live?

Our current moment is an interesting one from which to consider what *democracy* actually means—and how it has been manipulated, abused, and stretched wildly out of its original shape and form.

In looking for answers, the film takes a perambulatory approach, wandering from Athenian olive groves to Floridian beaches and including an array of different folk, including Cornel West, Eleni Perdikouri, Silvia Federici, and George Papandreou (the former prime minister of Greece). Along the way, different ideas, interpretations, experiences and ideologies are held up to the light. And by that I mean talked about.

The choice not to impose an overriding, omniscient narrative makes the film as democratic as its subject in presenting "different kinds of intellectual authority," in the words of the filmmaker. As a result, Taylor has created a true essay film, in the classic sense of the word's meaning: an attempt to figure shit out. If ever shit needed figuring out, it is now. As she notes: "Everywhere you look, democracy is in trouble."

In examining how we came to be where we are, the film goes back to the creation of both the first democratic state and Plato's *Republic*. But even Plato was not sure democracy stood a chance, built as it was on fractious, contrarian human nature—there never was a great idea that humans couldn't mess up.

As philosopher Eleni Perdikouri states in the film, it all began with the question of happiness. "What makes a life worth living?" she asks. She says that for the ancient Greeks, a good life meant a good, unified city with justice for all. But even at the very invention of democracy, a snake lurked in the garden. Plato saw wealth and its counterpart, poverty, as threats to the vision of a good city. Perdikouri explains that rich people want to become richer and split the city into rich and poor, which leads to civil war and sows the seeds for tyranny. "Poor people will follow any demagogue who will promise to overthrow the rich," she notes.

Right on cue, up pops the yam-coloured potus, declaring, "Ruled by the people, folks!" Following Donald Trump's appearance is a painfully on-point Platonic quote: "The greatest penalty for declining to rule is to be ruled by someone worse than oneself."

But the question that the film keeps circling back to is whether people are really made to rule themselves. The narrative turns in a widening gyre, collecting opinions, contradictions, and paradoxes—Rousseauian, Dostoevskyian, and Platonic—into a whirlwind. As Cornel West says, "Plato's challenge will never go away." As West describes it, the concept of democracy flies in the face of evidence that suggests people aren't good at self-rule. "The burden is simply too great. West talks about how social change does not come from majority rule, saying school desegregation in the United States would never have come about without some dictatorial force being applied. Going up against so many examples from human history to argue democracy can work may sometimes feel foolish. But as West says with a pirate's grin, "Count me in the crowd of the holy fools!"

In the debate about what constitutes true democracy, Taylor folds in conversations with philosophers, academics, and activists but gives equal weight to ordinary folk. Scenes of West in full verbal flight are laid next to a group of high school kids talking about their struggle to get a hot lunch. A barber who served a nine-year prison sentence speaks with startling clarity and erudition about what it means to observe society from a cage.

Out of this juxtaposition comes something fully alive. The darkness between arguments—the pause, the void, the uncertainty—animates Taylor's film. It doesn't claim to have the answers, and although there is the occasional grand polemic, mostly it involves the slow process of exchange and inquiry.

Some of these question-and-answer sessions go better than others. In the bright Miami sunshine, a group of ordinary people are assembled on a park bench and asked a series of questions:

"Do you live in a democracy?"

"Yes!"

"Do you vote?"

"No!"

There you have it—Rousseau's Paradox in the flesh, or as philosopher Wendy Brown asks, "How do you make democracy out of an undemocratic people?" Brown asserts that democracy does not come naturally but must be actively cultivated. But the forces ranged against the idea of collective self-determination are enormous and global in scope, whereas democracy is rooted in place and people. It doesn't seem a fair fight, and perhaps it really isn't.

"What we see today, I think, is a strong temptation to just turn the whole business of governing over to the technocrats," Brown says. "Not just to corporations, not just the wealthy, but to essentially human versions of algorithms.... Or algorithms themselves." The result is a world largely ruled by profit, and loss and by what enhances value and depreciates value. "It's a very narrow universe of thought and of conduct.... I find that terrifying," she says.

Plato's warning that economic disparity inevitably leads to tyranny takes on an even more ominous scope when considering global capitalism. What counters globalized capital, but globalized democracy? But whether that is even possible remains to be seen.

Still, Taylor's film is alive with febrile hope, offering not only wrangling, tangling debate, but real situations, lived experience, and democracy in the raw. Even as the social body is sawn apart, there are people working to stitch it back together again. Often these are folks who have been historically left out of the discussion—women, people of colour, LGBTQ2S+ people, and little kids.

In *What Is Democracy?* genuine action happens not in the Oval Office or a UN conference room but in makeshift medical centres that sprang up in Greece under austerity measures, a workers' co-op that employs refugees from across Latin America, or a living room in Miami where young activists debate who gets to be a citizen, whether mobility is more important than capital, and ultimately, "Who gets to count and who gets counted?

The spot fires of real democratic change are burning hotly in the polling booths, with the Voting Rights Act in the US under attack by those who want to disenfranchise minorities and the poor. As Henry "Mickey" Michaux Jr., who worked with Martin Luther King Jr., bluntly states in the North Carolina General Assembly, "The Klan now dresses up in suits and vests." He goes on to say there is not a single person of colour in the Republican caucus in North Carolina. The incestuous mingling of money and power hasn't changed much since the times of slavery, but voter-suppression laws constitute a new assault on the very heart of democracy.

As oligarchic money, power, and influence work to dismantle US democracy, it is an increasingly ugly and violent struggle. Following protests over a police shooting in Charlotte, North Carolina, a young activist named Delaney Vandergrift describes a white man getting out of his car and pointing a gun at the crowd. Vandergrift is asked, "What does democracy feel like?" She answers, "It doesn't feel like being scared for my life."

In one of the film's most startling scenes, a trio of emergency room surgeons talk about the reality of treating unending waves of trauma victims in a large Miami hospital. One surgeon notes that the us Army sends its medics for pre-deployment training to that hospital in Miami, as there is more trauma in Miami than in an active combat zone. The doctor then adds, "Trauma is a political disease."

The despair that comes from poverty is also about disparity, with extreme wealth right next to extreme poverty. This kind of inequality leads to increased violence, soaring homicide rates, and poor health. It is also not accidental, with democratic governments being co-opted by corporations. Asked how to cure the social body, the doctors answer as one: "Education from the very beginning." But even that is not without complexities. In fact, it is where the struggle begins between those who have power and those who have none.

As Taylor notes, "Public education is both a social leveller and enforcer of vast proportions." The film includes a discussion with a group of high school kids who, when asked about how they feel about their ability to have a say in their lives, are very clear about the fact that people who talk back or demand change are punished. As one young girl says, "I don't think people in a higher power really want to hear from a black mom in the ghetto."

But as the debate erupts about the kids' struggle to get a warm lunch at school, something very interesting happens: we witness a birth of collective action. The kids take apart the hypocrisy of the adults around them, resulting in a spontaneous round of applause and shy smiles from the young firebrands around the table. Suddenly, they are united and self-organizing—a fighting unit for social change and hot food!

There it is, folks—*demos* (people) *cratia* (power) in the flesh, a far cry, as Taylor points out, from Thomas Carlyle's theory that "great men both make and break history."

But the old, white men are holding on tight. Recent high-profile documentaries were largely about white men such as Steve Bannon (*American Dharma*), Donald Trump (*Fahrenheit 11/9*), Vladimir Putin (*Putin's Witnesses*), and Mikhail Gorbachev (*Meeting Gorbachev*) — all made by male filmmakers (Errol Morris, Michael Moore, Frederick Wiseman, and Werner Herzog, respectively). Purely by existing, Taylor's work is already a radical departure from the mainstream. But more importantly, she is unafraid to linger in uncertainty, and in this, she shares a lot in common with film essayist Chris Marker, in particular his legendary series *The Owl's Legacy*. It's an ongoing process, this democratic experiment. "That's what Plato was also complaining about," she says. "Not much has changed in human nature." Everything that humans create contains the seeds of its own destruction. From its beginning, the democratic experiment was predicated on slavery. As Cornel West explains, "Athens was a slave-based democracy. The United States, a slave-based democracy . . ."

But in the United States, race and power remain an open wound. In a stentorian speech, Angela Davis talks about how the system cannot be fixed as slavery was never fully abolished in the United States—it simply changed form. She argues that a very different kind of democracy is needed from that first version established by the founding white fathers, and that it remains the challenge of the 21st century.

It is a point reiterated by a young black barber, Ellie Brett, who talks about the experience of prison as little more than state-sanctioned slavery. "I did nine years. . . . I worked in a meat plant. You get paid what they call an incentive wage, forty cents a day." The humiliation of cuffs and collar is one thing, but the insidious effects of incarceration go bone deep. "You're not worthy enough of human contact. That's what missing—trying to getting guys like me to acclimate to society . . . so that we can survive," Brett says. "I can't live or work because I messed up ten years ago?" Astra Taylor interjects, "You also can't vote, right?"

Brett is sanguine about his experience, but underneath you can see the pain on the verge of spilling out and over. "I think that democracy is inherently flawed because people have to act it out," he says. "Like Machiavelli said, Man is a sorry breed, they're selfish and greedy, they're like parasites. . . . I'm sitting in a cage, looking at it. What are you going to do about it? You gotta fight." Ellis talks about being involved in hunger strikes that started after prison officials tried to take away the library. "This lady came, and she told us no one can go to school anymore—y'all don't deserve to get an education. So we stood up and fight."

As philosopher Wendy Brown says, "To have a democracy, there has to be a *we*—you have to know who 'we the people' are." That also means some people are excluded, and historically, that exclusion has been based on race, gender, and economic status, naming who's human and who's not. But the nightmare of our time, she suggests, is that antidemocratic forces are now supranational and globalized, whereas "democracy is still operating on a grounded and spatialized domain."

But globalism can also work for the continuation and expansion of the democratic struggle. Cornel West argues that change reverberates, echoing out like a thunderclap. "Real signs of freedom, struggle. Other folk gonna pick up on this . . . . The enslaved people will, the workers will, the women will, the gay and lesbian brothers and sisters will, the transgender folk, the bisexual folk, all will pick up on this. Lo and behold! This is a human affair, but what does it mean? It means from the very beginning, this is a global affair! . . . All of these arbitrary boundaries, all of these lines of demarcation, these walls that separate, are shattered," he says. "All those precious folk have exactly the same values, and that's a very different way of looking at the world."

The people rule. Not from above, always from below. As Taylor's film peels back the layers, stripping the thing down to bare studs and wires to reveal the foundations upon which the entire structure is built, something else begins to emerge.

Hope seems too soft a term, as there something stubborn, flinty almost, in people's dedication to the idea of democracy. It is there in the kids applauding one of their own speaking truth to power. It is amply evident in the intelligence, warmth, and gentleness that beams out of Silvia Federici like a corona. It is there in the heated, impassioned discussion in a grad student's living room as people of all colours come together to declare that all lives matter. The idea is big enough to contain a world of opinions, contradiction and paradoxes.

What is Democracy? is a call to arms, but it is also a powerful and piercing reminder of Plato's dictum, "Nothing beautiful without struggle." In fact, the struggle may be the most important part.

A version of this essay was published online at the Tyee *(thetyee.ca).*

CHAPTER THREE

Alighted

To gather
To become
Is becoming
Radiant
    breath is never alone
She wanted to tell us all
she felt
Intimacy longing
All she had
Breaking.

She waited
for you, for all of us
delighting in anticipation
breathing she begins
To erupt.

— carla bergman

Lilac Tree

Born deep under a lilac tree
at Brockton Point
to the spirits of longshoremen;
She belongs to a nation of
children flying
dreams in skies
claimed by military men.

Ghosts in battledress,
who stole her mother tongue
and her father's identity;
They never get enough.
Nevertheless, she knows
where she's from.

Now a soft boy gives her love
in vain. A soft boy
waits in the shadows
of a lilac tree.
But her heart is with her revolution.

She fights in a language
that's not her own
to protect boys
who are not her sons,
from the impressions of wildcats and warriors;
From the sound of her
dying lilac tree.

—Jamie-Leigh Gonzales

EMMA Talks Community-Engaged Art Practice

Corin Browne

Whenever a new project comes my way, I ask myself two questions: Is it joyful? and Is it raising a ruckus? I have never constructed boundaries between my parenting, academic life, activism, career, and desire to build a community I want to live in. So over the years, I have learned to craft projects with potential for joy—for myself and the folks I work with. The road to joy is usually emotionally exhausting, creatively challenging, and technically rigorous, but in my experience, it is filled with the kind of happiness only hope, imagination, and the creation of new friendships can ignite.

Raising a ruckus is about making noise that disturbs. It asks us to question the world we live in: What is justice? Where do we belong? How do we create change? When carla pitched EMMA Talks to me in 2014, I knew it would fulfill both my criteria. I said yes before she even finished describing her vision. Joyful? What could be more profoundly joyful than carving out space for women to share stories in and spreading those stories online? And ruckus? I knew carla would invite speakers with stories so powerful and important we would feel their impact for years.

After the first EMMA Talk in 2015, carla and I realized we also wanted to expand EMMA, a space for self-identified women to speak, to also include artmaking as a way to build community before and after each talk. I have been a practising community-engaged artist for over fifteen years, often in

collaboration with my dear friend Patti Fraser. Something incredibly profound happens when people gather to make art together. When creativity
happens in a community-engaged context facilitated by an artist, it can be
truly transformative. I have been lucky to carve out a career of paid work
that is immensely joyful and rooted in social justice. I was eager to see
how that experience could intersect with EMMA Talks.

Before EMMA, my work as a community-engaged artist was predicated
on deep, long-term relationships. My most meaningful projects were slow
building and long term, unfolding over many years. I struggled with the
impact that each EMMA event would make as a singular art engagement.
Who was the community? Would we need to rebuild it every EMMA, or
would we see a community build around the talks? We wanted diverse
speakers, which meant our audience would shift each event. With a new
issue and new audience every time, would it still feel like a genuinely
engaged community art process? How could artists build community in
this context? Would the short time allow meaningful work to be produced?

We decided to work *with* the tensions of these questions and to trust
that a new art engagement could emerge. We acknowledged that the
strongest community-engaged art projects are sustained, long-term projects that allow relationships to build over time, but we hoped that this
type of experiment would build a strong, vibrant community surrounding
the Talks anyway.

With the financial support of the BC Arts Council and the City of
Vancouver, we contracted several artists to produce collaborative art-based
events exploring each talk's themes. We envisioned the art engagements
would allow EMMA audience members to, among themselves, continue
conversations already begun by EMMA speakers. We also wanted to transform conventional audience–speaker dynamics by enabling new dialogue
interactions and possibilities. Many of our speakers, freed from the social
expectations typical of receptions and question-and-answer periods,
participated in the art making, too. Most importantly, we hoped to explore
the possibilities of collaborative art making as a community response to
important issues and ideas.

Our first event featured emerging community-engaged artists Sylvia McFadden and Vivienne McMaster. Their beautiful "Thoughtful Photobooth" created opportunities for the EMMA audience to explore self-portraiture and digital responses linked to quotes from the talk. We then collaborated with Vanessa Richards, who led our audience in powerful participatory song before and after Rebecca Solnit's talk.

We shifted gears in spring 2016 to collaborate with Caroline Ballhorn and Jenny Lee Craig of Tin Can Studio to create a multi-event artist residency. Jenny and Caroline explored the theme of connection through the metaphor of thread, a participatory art piece using that theme, the creation of a protest banner, public letter writing to politicians, and igniting conversation and communication by encouraging audience members to make buttons that would act as an invitation for talking points with each other.

In 2017, we worked with guest curator Michelle Nahanee to plan an EMMA Talk with Squamish women. Michelle also curated an art engagement piece for the night that explored the connections between art, play, and performance through her life-sized board game, Sínulkhay and Ladders, and "decolonizing activity book for the woke and the weary." Michelle's incredible work was the final of our seven art engagements, to date.

This experiment expanded my definition of community-engaged art practice. I will continue seeking long-term, slow-building projects. The art engagements, though, embodied our goal to create open and convivial spaces so folks across difference could find common ground. In the spirit of noise making and joyful creation, I hope we increased recognition of community-engaged art practices as meaningful, vital forms of artistic collaboration and expression.

Lost Lagoon

The morning air, moist with tree tears,
wets my cheeks as I walk near
the water's edge.
Drawing a sharp cold breath,
I know,
winter is coming
to
Lost Lagoon.

Distant traffic, silenced by fog
and the pounding of my heart.
Footprints on footprints,
my circle mandala.
Slow down,
gold leaves of autumn
and
chilling waters.

I am safe here, my soul lives here
beneath tree canopies.
The cedar's musk comforts
for the trees, like my kin,
call me,
time to come home now,
to
my heartland.

Cathedral trees, Seven Sisters
One still feels their presence
visiting their gravesite.
Majestic tree mothers,
now gone,
fallen long ago,
yet
still nurture.

Many grand dames lost along the path
now lay in mossy graves,
supporting younger trees.
Family values live on,
life lessons.
Kin, not kindling.
My
re-kindling.

Beyond the park, my family weeps.
Machines now switched off.
Soon too, will my brother.
I see him in this wood,
mossy bed.
Us nursing, holding
to
thoughts of him.

They have gathered, some from afar
as if pulled by long threads
to weave tight knit comfort,
around breaking hearts,
hold on.
We are together.
Soon,
hold tighter.

The lagoon ripples, the mist lifts

and a swan swims in view.
Skirting the shore, seeking
her nest and I think of
Mother
connecting our threads.
Fall
Winter's near.

Wet cheeks sting in the cold air and
sisters now pull my thread.
Hurry, hurry downtown.
Push the door open, hush,
waiting
The circle opens
and
I weave in.

Gathered together my family
listening, gasps for breath,
foretelling loss and pain.
Sisters strong embrace
rooted.
He is falling now.
Soft
bed of moss.

A wind blows hard, trees leaning in
Five sisters, Five brothers
Mother, kin, our family tree
Braced against the cold, and
I know,
winter has come
to
Lost Lagoon.

—Julie Martin

ABOVE AND FACING PAGE Pre-talks reception.

TOP LEFT The Love Doctor, by Tasnim Nathoo.

TOP RIGHT, MIDDLE LEFT, AND BOTTOM Local artists selling their works at EMMA Talks.

RIGHT, TOP TO BOTTOM Thoughtful Photobooth, with Sylvia McFadden and Vivienne McMaster

Participatory Song with Vanessa Richards

Participatory Song with Vanessa Richards

WORDS CAN BE A POWERFUL MOTIVATOR FOR ACTION

What message would you like to see amplified?

Come weave together and celebrate our collective voice.

For the next three EMMA Talks, we will be creating a woven weatherproof banner that can be used at public events - community gatherings, rallies, marches, protests - anywhere a crowd is gathered.

We would like to decide what our banner will say with all of you who have come here tonight. You are invited to contribute ideas on post-it notes and stick them to the grey board. It could be a call to action, a message of inspiration, a symbol, a hashtag, a line from a poem or song... we are excited to see what inspires you and what messages you think are worth sharing.

We will also work on the backdrop for our banner. Grab some recycled tarp strips and help us weave them together to create a base for our message. The tarp material we are re-using was damaged and could no longer serve it's original intention, we are happy to give it another life through this participatory art project!

At the next EMMA Talk, we will be back and will start to add the message to the banner.

We welcome comments and feedback - please feel free to reach out to hello@tincanstudio.org.

Tin Can Studio's Year-Long Residency at EMMA Talks

ABOVE AND FACING PAGE Common Threads, part of the Tin Can Studio
Year-Long Residency at EMMA Talks

MIDDLE Jenny Lee Craig and Caroline Ballhorn of Tin Can Studio

ABOVE AND FACING PAGE, TOP Playing Sínulkhay and Ladders with Michelle Nahanee

Decolonizing activity book for the "woke and the weary"

CHAPTER FOUR

Ascending

Her song is like a knife
because
   Silencing.
Generations of whispers
cutting through
all
the haze
listen for it
Territories shifting
crack
     crack
        crack
Voices breaking
Fault lines under the stars
through the mist
Thundering begins
never ending
because
there is much to recover

—carla bergman

I'm Afraid of Men

Vivek Shraya

I'M AFRAID OF MEN because it was men who taught me fear.

I'm afraid of men because it was men who taught me to fear the word *girl* by turning it into a weapon they used to hurt me. I'm afraid of men because it was men who taught me to hate and eventually destroy my femininity. I'm afraid of men because it was men who taught me to fear the extraordinary parts of myself.

My fear was so acute that it took almost two decades to undo the damage of rejecting my femininity, to salvage and reclaim my girlhood. Even now, after coming out as a trans girl, I am more afraid than ever. This fear governs many of the choices I make, from the beginning of my day to the end.

In the morning, as I get ready for work, I avoid choosing clothes or accessories that will highlight my femininity and draw unwanted attention. On the hierarchy of harassment, staring is the least violent consequence for my gender nonconformity that I could hope for. And yet the experience of repeatedly being stared at has slowly mutated me into an alien.

If I decide to wear tight pants, I walk quickly to my bus stop to avoid being seen by the construction workers outside my building, who might shout at me as they have on other mornings.

When I'm on a packed bus or streetcar, I avoid making eye contact with men, so that no man will think I might be attracted to him and won't be able to resist the urge to act upon this attraction. I squeeze my shoulders inward if a man sits next to me, so that I don't accidentally touch him.

If I open Twitter or Facebook on the way to work, I brace myself for news reports of violence against women and gender-nonconforming people, whether it's a story about another trans woman of colour who has been murdered, or the missing and murdered Indigenous women, or sexual assault. As important as it is to make these incidents visible by reporting them, sensationalizing and digesting these stories is also a form of social control, a reminder that I need to be afraid and to try to be as invisible as possible.

Despite the authority I have as a teacher, I'm embarrassed any time a cluster of male students laughs in my classroom, fearing that I might be their joke. As a result, I often deploy self-deprecating humour throughout my lessons—if I make myself the punchline, their laughter will sting less. My hyperawareness of the men in my class, and the fact that male students tend to speak up more in discussions, make me prone to learning their names first. How might this recognition of men, however fear-based, contribute to their overall success? I leave every class repeating the names of my female students (especially the names of my racialized female students) in an effort to combat this ingrained sexism. I also become nervous when a male student asks to meet with me to challenge a grade, fearful he'll get loud or even hit me when we're alone in my office.

Beyond managing this fear, I must also monitor how it might inadvertently result in preferential treatment.

When I have to send emails to men, including male colleagues and artists, I carefully compose each message and include several exclamation marks.

> Hi Jim!
> Hope you are well! Just following up on my message from two weeks ago about the broken cupboard in my unit!
> Please let me know when you have time to take a look!
> Thank you!
> VS

Exclamation marks soften my message, modifying my tone so that my words convey the requisite submissiveness to communicate effectively with a man, to avoid agitating or offending him. I am not allowed to be assertive or direct.

When I walk to lunch and hear a man walking behind me, I move to the edge of the sidewalk so that he can pass. I used to speed up, but no matter how much I quickened my stride, I couldn't escape my anxiety. Men tend to drag their feet on the concrete, asserting their presence both spatially and sonically. But when I check over my shoulder, no one is there. I've grown fearful of any rustle behind me.

If I have an errand at a music or camera store, I make sure I've done my research beforehand, so that I won't have to ask one of the shaggy, bearded male staff members chatting among themselves to assist me or weather their condescension if I don't know the right model number or am unfamiliar with a particular setting. Or I just ask my boyfriend to buy my guitar strings for me. The snobbish, superior attitudes of such men have prevented me from calling myself a musician for years, even though I write songs, record albums, and tour.

When I arrive at home after work and the elevator reaches my floor, I wait to get off last so that I won't be trapped in the hallway with a man behind me, in case he tries to push me.

If I have no choice but to get off first, I rush to my apartment, chased by a ghost. I dread every time I see a notice on my door, expecting it to say FAGGOT.

If I head back out in the evening for a gig, I wait in my apartment, ear to the door, until I'm sure there's no one in the hallway, to avoid running into my bro neighbours while I'm red-lipped and gold-adorned. Or I ask my boyfriend to walk me to the main entrance of our building. Before Uber, I would ask him to walk me to the street and help me hail a cab. I realized only after I began transitioning that my lifetime of independence and self-reliance had been largely a result of male privilege. Being a girl has required me to retrain myself to think of depending on others or asking for assistance not as weakness or even as pathetic, but rather as a necessity.

I pay attention to the app to see which direction the Uber will arrive from and I face the other way, so the driver won't be able to see me from afar and drive away, as some have done. As I wait, I blur my vision so that I don't notice strangers gawking at me as they walk by.

Once inside the car, I try to look preoccupied with my phone to avoid any nasty interaction with the driver that could include degrading comments about women—a recurring and disturbing pattern in my life.

"How about them oriental chicks?"

"You can tell it's summer by all the girls running around in short dresses."

"Last week, I had a mother in the back seat and a daughter in the front, and I could smell the daughter's fresh pussy."

This is how drivers attempt to reconcile their discomfort with my gender—by aggressively asserting their masculinity. First, they "man" me, robbing me of my femininity and turning me into one of their bros, and then they share their oversexualized opinions about women and girls. I've even had a cab driver hand me a plastic bag of garbage and ask me to take it out. Was this his way of telling me that I, too, am trash?

When I'm at sound check, I say "testing, testing" a couple of times into the mic, maybe sing a phrase or two, and then finish. I don't ask for my monitor, my vocal mic, or my audio track to be turned up or down. I wouldn't dare ask for reverb. I don't ask for anything for fear that the soundman will start grunting, swearing, or making disparaging comments about how I am playing "laptop music," code for mock music.

I carry makeup wipes to all my gigs so that I can quickly "take off my face," as I say to my friends, before I leave the relative safety of the performance venue. The saddest part of the night is when I peel my bindi off my forehead and let it fly into the wind, a symbolic parting with a piece of myself.

My fear of men is a fuel that both protects my body, as a survival instinct, and erodes it, from overuse. Since coming out as trans, I have been stricken with numerous freak pains and repetitive strain injuries that practitioners are unable to explain or cure. When they suspiciously ask me, "Are you sure nothing happened? You didn't fall somewhere?" I want to respond, "I live in fear."

The only time I can make choices about how I want to look, act, communicate is when I'm inside my apartment, at the end of the day. Often exhausted, I try my best not to think about how I will have to do it all over again tomorrow.

The weight of these minute-to-minute compromises is compounded by the fact that because of my fear of violence from men, I seldom dress the way I want to in public and wear makeup only on weekends or when I'm performing. This means I'm often still seen as a man.

As painful as it is to be seen as the embodiment of my fears, the real agony comes from feeling that I am to blame because I don't look feminine enough. When I finally accepted that the only way I could stop my male classmates from tormenting me for being too girly was by pretending to be a boy, I knew I couldn't afford to be just an average boy. In my mind, the better I performed my new role, the safer I would be. In order to survive childhood, I became an exceptional boy. So now, when I'm seen as male, there's a part of me that worries that it's my fault—for having striven to be the perfect man, and for having excelled at it.

Although I've paid a high price for that proficiency, I learned a great deal from the years I spent observing men and creating my own version of manhood. I've also endured the added challenge of being attracted to men in spite of my fears. These experiences place me, a queer trans girl, in a unique position to address what actually makes a good man, and how we can reimagine forms of masculinity that don't arouse fear.

What I Know About My Brother

Walidah Imarisha

Kakamia created a piece of art, a bio/prose/poem hybrid, "Frayed Subconscious." A handkerchief, stained in paint, kisses and rips of ink. He told me it was part of the evidence against him, and it was. Perhaps it was not evidence from his legal trial, but it was evidence by the state, brought against him at the time of his birth, and at the time of his indictment. The poetic vulnerable masculinity of the piece was part of the mounting case that would eventually sentence him to life in poverty: a life in racism, a life spent more behind prison walls than outside of them.

"This handkerchief was the last piece of freedom," the art piece reads. "It held the forensics to convict and heard the whispers of innocence to acquit a 16-year-old accused hit man. It traveled through county jails, courthouses and state prisons. It consoled the fears of California's most infamous criminals and masterminds, and has soaked up the blood of prison riot victims."

Poetry can exquisitely change lives. It can sustain life in the worst of circumstances. And all poetry is a lie. Facts are not poetic enough to reveal the rhythm of a human heart. We thank poetry for its inaccuracies—imperfect cracks on the face of beauty through which the light is able to shine through—word to poet Leonard Cohen.

So when Kakamia told me he met Mac in New York—whom he called his godfather—through his uncle who had connections to the Westies and numbers rackets, I understood the need to create ties and community. When

Kakamia said he would leave his Crown Heights, Brooklyn neighborhood to run errands for his uncle, I understood the desire in him to be tied to something more powerful, more terrifying, than his own thin brown body.

I asked Mac about my brother the first time I met him.

"Great kid," he replied, beaming. "He's got a good heart, Kakamia does."

Kakamia was man of a thousand names as well. Names are a precious and powerful part of your identity. Knowing a name means you have a piece of that person. He had his birth name, signifying the child who continued getting up, mouth tasting like dirt and metal, when life knocked him to the ground. A prison ID number, an absence of self so a system can get on with its business of making commodities out of human beings without guilt. He was known as "New York" to people a continent away, where a Puerto Rican was a novelty item. "New York" shared in the cool of power, tinged with danger, that the city embodied. He was Kakamia Jahad Imarisha to those who wanted to see the man he so desperately tried to be, the man that, most of the time, he succeeded in being.

"Have you seen his art?" Mac continued, "Phenomenal, just amazing. I wish I could draw like that, I'm telling you."

"Was he always like that?" I asked tentatively, eggshells crunching under my voice. "Was he like that in New York?"

"Oh I didn't know him in New York. I only met him when I came out here. But we've known each other a long time out here. He's a really good kid, not like some of these knuckleheads around here.

I have come to learn everything I need of the truth I have now. It lives in my brother's eyes, in his strong talented hands flaked by sun and harsh soap. I gather pieces of my brother's truth and string them like beads to create a necklace, a talisman of protection.

....

I know prison is harsh, brutal, soul-crushing, and above all monotonous. The sheer boredom of being trapped with the same people every day, of having limited options—do I watch TV, listen to music, work out, write a letter, read a book, then do it all again tomorrow?

A prisoner told me upon his release, "It's not the guards that got to me—I learned to shut myself off from them. It wasn't the other inmates; most of them were cool and you learn early how to avoid the ones who aren't. What got me lying in my bunk at night—staring at the ceiling scrawled with drawings and messages from past prisoners—was knowing that I had to get up and do the same thing every day, for 2,237 days. That's when I felt myself slipping away: when I thought of it like that."

I know my brother's body is landscaped with tattoos.

You can read his history, lived and reimagined, on his skin. He is a book written by an illegal prison ink gun made out of a hollowed-out broken pen tube, a needle pricked into one end. Blood clots around every word and image.

A grim reaper, scythe in hand, dominates his left arm. From his gang days he told me, when he was "Mr. Grim." I have a picture of him at his junior prom. He is 15 years old, body jutting out at all the awkward angles of that age, stuffed into a black tuxedo with a pink cummerbund and tie, to match his date's Cinderella dress. His arms are wrapped around her, and his square jaw juts forward with a toothy grin. Her eyes dancing with a pink smile that matches the bows in her curly hair. I stare at this picture and wonder if the grim reaper is there as well, swathed in the pink cummerbund. Is he smiling for the picture too?

Bruce Lee is on his leg—"That's one baaaaaad nigga!" Kakamia bellowed. He was completely unfazed when I reminded him Bruce, though amazing, was in fact Chinese, and also he should stop using the word "nigga" so much.

Another tattoo features an amateurish portrait of the rapper Da Brat, a now-forgotten splash in the pop culture pool. The original ink bled; the tattoo has faded over the twenty years it has lived on his skin. "Yeah, it's gotten all fucked up . . . I'm gonna get that covered up; I just gotta come up with something," he mused.

Like his life, he revises his tattoos, keeping the images and ink that still breathe true, and erasing facts that have turned into lies through the insistent passage of time.

Many of my brother's tattoos have come after his incarceration. It is illegal for prisoners to tattoo themselves. I have met multiple men that have let my brother paint their flesh while on the inside. Some prison tats are crude and simplistic. Others, like Kakamia's, are elegant and full of life. Kakamia brings the lightest part of him to his work, his imagination skimming their skin: sunlight on a warm lake.

Kakamia does his own tattoos when the only other tattoo artist he trusts gets sent to the hole. He feels the bite of the needle, creating hours of tedium where attention cannot wander, the stinging kiss a penance and a gift.

He bleeds for his art. He bleeds to remake himself.

The ink is created from a ballpoint pen if you want the quick and dirty way. The "professional" prison ink is composed of soot from burning toilet paper, wood, Styrofoam, and something like black chess pieces. These are mixed with rubbing alcohol and water; small stones are added in the mixing process. It is the introduction of extreme heat that pushes a metamorphosis to occur. This furtive prison cell. This chemistry experiment is more complex than any class tests I conducted in college courses.

The expanse of Kakamia's skin has become crowded with the remains of things burnt. It is full body armor: arms to back, legs to tops of feet. Ivy curls around fingers, the eyes of a portrait of a political martyr stare out of the top of Kakamia's skull. The martyr chose death over jail. *When I die, I wear nothing but the tats on my back.* From his poem "Last Stand." The tat on his back screams, "Fuck the World" across his shoulder blades in Old English (malt) lettering.

Almost a decade ago, doctors cut out cancer that had settled near his heart, two inches under his right nipple. It had been growing in him for some time, they said—it was just now big enough to notice. They do not know how he got cancer. "The environment you grew up in probably contained toxins in large quantities," the doctor said, telling him something he knew his entire life. His whole life has been carcinogenic.

His scar is camouflaged by the West African Adinkra symbol for eternal energy. Kakamia no longer hides his scars, but paints them brightly.

In the middle of his chest is a bullseye, and an edict: "No warning shots."

Kakamia has the symbol for the revolutionary Puerto Rican indepentistas, Los Macheteros, swaddling his Adam's apple. Their blood-red star has a machete through it, surrounded by an outline of the island of Puerto Rico.

"Cuz you know how your hermano get down!" he shouted joyfully the first time I saw it.

Kakamia and I share a tattoo—his at the base of his neck, Adinkra symbol for change and adaptability, mine on my left shoulder. It was the first tattoo I ever got, a reminder to me not to fear what the future brings—that change is constant, and rigidity is the enemy. The tattoo is a reminder to Kakamia that such a thing as change exists beyond the same three walls and set of barred teeth greeting his eyes every day. As sci fi writer Octavia Butler wrote, "*God is change.*"

I do not believe in god. I struggle to believe in change. When I got my tattoo I was terrified. I wasn't scared of leaving permanent marks on my body—the multiple cigarette burns and shallow razor slashes on my forearms, breasts, and abdomen were evidence of that. When I pushed the smoldering mouth of the cigarette to my skin, it was power I smelled burning. That was pain I could control as a teenager: scars I chose to carry rather than those that had been forced upon me. I was scared of uncontrollable pain.

In the tattoo parlor, I shook in the chair. The woman, covered almost completely in dayglo tattoos and endless piercings, readied her instruments. My friend was there, holding my hand, breathing for me. I had planned the design small, slightly larger than a dime, stacking the odds in my favor of making it through.

"You ready?" the artist asked, needle already purring.

The first kiss was like the sensual gnawing of my first lover's teeth on my skin.

"Is that it?" I asked her, incredulous.

"Yep, that's as bad as it's going to get," she said over the hum of my identity being etched onto me. I started laughing.

Kakamia loves to tell the story of me laughing through my first tattoo. It proves how tough and baaaad his little sister is. Like Bruce Lee.

"See, now we're connected by ink."

Kakamia has a portrait of me tattooed over his heart, two afro puffs perched like dark planets on the side of my head. I have seen a photograph of this tattoo. I am not allowed to see the tattoo itself, of course, because we only meet in visiting rooms, under the watchful eyes of guards.

I hate the picture of me he chose. Taken in my friend's car when I was 18, I was preparing to step out into the rain, back into my apartment, into the relationship I wanted so desperately to escape—the one I finally did escape—with a bruised wrist and a fear of eyes watching me through windows. I turned to say goodbye and got a face full of flash. The picture is a torn girl trying to paste herself into a woman, all unfinished edges and messy wet glue.

I love living on my brother's skin; I just wish it was a wholer me that resided there.

Kakamia's name is a bracelet encompassing the span of my wrist. My third tattoo and my last. So far. A birthday surprise for Kakamia. After he immortalized me on his skin, every time we would talk, he would joke, "So when you getting my face tattooed on you? Only fair you know."

I did not want his face frozen. It would be only one of the countless hims I have seen over the years. It would be a fact, and it would be a lie.

So I chose words, as I always have: the letters I gave him, strung together with poetry.

I ventured deep into North Philly to an art studio, up rickety, dusty stairs to a room plastered with pin-up girls on cars and death metal bands thrusting their manhood out. The artist was a dreadlocked Black man with heavy eyes, I hoped, from lack of sleep and not weed.

He tried to talk to me while I gritted my teeth, the needle digging into the delicate bone of my wrist until it felt like sawing tendons. My boyfriend Dovid was with me. We had broken apart but we were still pretending to be whole, not so much for outsiders—they could all clearly see our cracks—but for ourselves. He put his hands on my shoulder and I jumped, causing a tiny line coming down from the second "a." Permanent. Like so many little mistakes.

On the next visit, I proudly rolled my sleeve back and held my illustrated wrist in front of Kakamia's face. These were ties more than blood: ties of choice.

He dragged me by my arm, showing everyone in the visiting room—prisoner, visitor and guard alike: "Look at that, that's my name, fool! I told y'all my baby sister loves her big brother, didn't I? Look at that, what did I tell you? That's my name!"

My brother was a graffiti artist, which is to say an outlaw. If you could read the wild styles of his youth, you could speak the words of the kamikaze graffiti tattoos on his flesh. Growing up in New York, where graf artists hung out of windows to put their names in gravity-defying places, Kakamia has become his own blank wall, readied for bombing (the graffiti term for covering a wall that isn't yours).

I can see him, tagging his name on walls, scaling fences into train yards to spend hours sucking in paint fumes, the only sounds the *shhhh* of the aerosol can, the rattle of the Krylon and your own hot breath in your ears. It is a way to leave your mark on the world: proof you were there. An undersized, skinny ghetto mule-atto mixed-up kid who never had enough money to get by. They can't erase you. Even if they sandblast you off, you'll come back. Immortality.

As he dragged me around and showed off my flesh, I was proud to realize I was his latest tag, his latest cry of resistance to a world intent on scrubbing him clean out of existence.

....

I know my brother is able to create joy in a place of sorrow. I know he is able to accept love as it is given, raw and unfinished, regardless of societal edicts.

At a time when intimacy between male prisoners is seen as either a violation or the punch line of a homophobic joke, my brother claims relationships with men, women, and trans folks.

This is not something prison engendered in him. In the 1980s, his desire was far too fluid for labels. In that climate and culture—which only had room for eithers—Kakamia transgressed all boundaries, and refused to live inside any box constructed for him.

Now, his body exists in a box constructed for him. But over the past twenty-five years, his heart has flown on broken angel wings to roost where it might find warmth.

He has found it with a transgender woman, Terra, housed in the same prison as Kakamia. She has a warrior spirit, sad eyes, and handwriting that looks like bubbles. Terra was a part of the fight that resulted in transgender prisoners at that facility receiving their hormones, hormones that allow them to look in the mirror and recognize the person they see when they look inward. "The denial of access to hormone treatment has profound effects, including extreme mental distress and anguish, often leading to an increased likelihood of suicide attempt, as well as depression, heart problems, and irregular blood pressure," according to *Queer Injustice: The Criminalization of LGBT People in the United States*. She knows all too personally what the denial of your ability to define yourself leads to.

Kakamia supported Terra in her work wholeheartedly, full of pride.

Terra and Kakamia are cellies, and have been for over a decade, at two different prisons. They have chosen to share space, to make a cell as much of a home as is possible. They have been many things to each other as the pressures of prison have caused fissures to flare up. They have not always been lovers as they are now—my brother is engaged to a woman on the outside—but Kakamia and Terra are always working to be loving to one another.

"Your brother drives me so crazy sometimes," the bubbles floated across Terra's lined notebook page. "He always thinks he's right, and he's so arrogant. I still love him, though."

A few months later, I received a large manila envelope from Kakamia. I unfurled a small canvas, splattered in deep rich colors. His artwork is beautiful and bold, and he has done many abstract paintings over the years. But I knew this was not his.

"This is her first attempt at a painting. I've been trying to get her to try for years, but she didn't think she'd be any good. Obviously she was wrong, which I told her already, 'cause this is great!" the accompanying note crowed.

"Anyway, she wanted you to have it. She knows you keep all of my artwork safe. She wanted her painting to live next to mine." Away from cell shakedowns and midnight prison transfers, away from the uncertainty of steel.

Excerpted from Angels with Dirty Faces: Three Stories of Crime, Prison, and Redemption, *published by AK Press, 2016.*

Excerpts from Mixed Vegetable

Anoushka Ratnarajah

QUEER HERE

Things actual white people, queer and straight, have said to me in real life:

Wow you're like the first lesbian Hindu I've ever met.

A gay Muslim?! Isn't that, like, impossible?

You don't meet many people like you who are gay.

Wow, that's so BRAVE.

It must be so hard for you.

It must have been so hard to come out to your family.

Have you told your family?

Did your family disown you?

It must be hard, lying to your family all the time.

You should tell them.

You're not being your true self.

You'll never be happy if you don't accept who you really are.

If they don't accept you, then you don't need them.

People over there are so homophobic.

We really need to educate those people.

It's too bad they don't know any better.

It's too bad your culture is so sexist.

I heard about those honour killings—that's so horrible! We're so lucky it's not like that in this country.

It must be so much easier for you to be queer here.

You must be so grateful you were born here.

It must be why you're a femme. It would be too hard to be butch back home.

You must have to go back into the closet when you're back home.

Do they even have gay people in your country?

Do they even have a word for gay in hindu?

You must be so grateful you're not trans because that would be even harder.

Women are so oppressed over there.

It must be so scary when you go back there.

It must be so hard not having any role models.

Do they even let you be gay over there?

Isn't it illegal to be gay in your country?

How do you, like, find other lesbians?

How many lesbians are there in India?

So is it, like, impossible to date over there?

It must be so sad—you can never get married!

How did you tell your parents you didn't want an arranged marriage?

So, would you, like, have a gay arranged marriage?

Oh, you should meet my friend, Priya/Shoba/Shalini/Amal/Kritika—she's gay too! I think you two would really hit it off.

Retorts:

I'm not a Hindu.

I'm not Muslim either.

I'm also not a lesbian.

My parents are actually fine with it.

It wasn't that hard.

I'm not lying to them.

Not all brown people are the same.

There are gay people in India.

There are probably plenty of lesbians in India.

I'm not actually from India.

I've only been to India once.

Hindu isn't a language.

Domestic violence happens everywhere.

I'm sure your friend is great.

Everything unsaid:

My mother is white. But her born-again Christian family—*my* born-again Christian family—doesn't think much of my "lifestyle."

It wasn't any harder to come out to them than it was to tell them I was raped.

You would have no idea where Sri Lanka is anyway.

I won't bother explaining Tamil either.

I'm a femme because I'm a femme. My gender isn't a result of my geographical location.

What do I tell you—that by default, circumstance, migration, colonialism, I have been looking up to white women all my life? That my sisters and I never crossed my own field of vision because you were all too bright and the lens had not adapted to capture me or us?

Yes, I was afraid when I went "back" to India for the first time. Yes, it was a familiar fear—of men, of brown men, of my otherness, of doing the wrong thing, of missing vocabulary, of myself.

You are the cause of my loneliness.

Dating is impossible because of you. Because you don't see a person.

I am not brave. I did not tell you this.

GATEWAY

You tell me I was your gateway

You're not my first
I've met so many versions of you
Best friend
Classmate
Co-worker
Collaborator
Co-organizer
Confidante
Casual fuck
Ambiguous gay hangout

I've been your
Best friend
Classmate
Co-worker
Collaborator
Co-organizer
Confidante
Casual fuck
Ambiguous gay hangout

Your teacher
Your experience
Your rite of passage
Your gateway

You tell me
I opened
The door
Your eyes
Your ears

Your mind
Your heart

I let you in
I opened
Made room

In my kitchen to feed you
On my bookshelf to learn you
In my bed to hold you
In my heart to love you
I opened
Sometimes only a crack
Sometimes swung so wide I could hear the hinges squeal
Gaping and rusted
Did you not hear it?
I thought it was so loud
I thought you were taking notes

You charted everything
Studied
Made maps
Graphs
Amateur cartographer

Put me in the back of your mind
Saved a corner in your heart for me to live in, under a sign that said
Good Person.

You thank me for being such a good teacher
Leave me an apple on my desk and steal gold stars from my desk drawers

You can leave
Only stay as long as you need me
As long as you want to

Eat your fill without reading the recipe or offering to clean up
Leave me the dishes and
Hungry
Tired
Cold

Your journey
Leaves marks
Inked crosses on the places that hold value
A treasure map for the next one of you to scavenge
X marks the spot

I see you stand in the light
Sheltered by your good intentions
Congratulated, adulated, applauded, lauded
Pat on the back
My back is your bridge across
An important stop on your journey
Because you are finished now
You have arrived
You have become
A good white person
You say all the right words
You surround yourself with other good white people
To talk
To collaborate
To love

And here I am
Sure that it's the last time
Bricking up the doorway
Until the next one comes along
So eager, so charming
Saying "I love you" in such a convincing tone

BALLET

When she was a young girl her mother sent her to ballet classes to educate her body on the proper way to express itself.

Her brown limbs were encased in pink elastic, a second skin to cover the shame of her own.

Pink like Barbie's plastic face. Pink like all the dolls she ever owned, relics of her mother's childhood with red curls and cold, pale cheeks. Her mother wouldn't buy her any new dolls. Girls' toys are expensive, and Barbie is a tool of the patriarchy.

So she played with her mother's playmates—pretended like she did. And the faces of her pretend children were not a match to her own but pink. Pink as her leotard and tights, which were pink like crayons she used to colour in paper faces at school, like the Band-Aids on her scraped knees, the red and brown crust of her broken self all the more obvious with the poor substitution of latex for skin.

Pink. Not beige. Pink was never beige, no matter how hard Crayola and Band-Aid might have tried. Pink was not beige, and beige was not brown.

To this day she still hates pastels.

Suck it in, suck it in, she was told, over and over, while all her friends were throwing up, vomiting, starving, cutting into that white skin she was so jealous of. She never understood why they wanted to disappear too. What did they have to be ashamed of?

Mind over matter. Put it into costume. Tell it to stand up straight. Eyes ahead. Suck it in, stop breathing and maybe you'll disappear, at last.

That was how she learned to dance.

ONLY ENGLISH

My father used to sing me a song to make me go to sleep
About a prince whose princess was stolen from him
He had to go rescue her
Rama
Sita

I remember thinking their names were so
Beautiful

He lifted me up
I put my head on his shoulder
How did the tune go?

I called him the other day
He can't remember the words either

He had no one to talk to
I don't know if he's lonely
If the words fight to escape
Underneath the weight of all the English he's had to carry since he was
a child
Falling asleep to that song we've both forgotten
I was small and safe
Now he's shrinking
What if he never sings that song again?

I want to be able to talk to him before he's gone
But by the time I learn,
Will he be beyond
remembering?
How long do our tongues hold on
to our cultures?
Will mine be stubborn
refuse
to wrap itself around the words
let them
slip off
dissolve in the air
the molecules
of my
history
broken
up

AUNTIES

"Sorry, only English," I say apologetically to my aunts the first time I meet them. To the drivers who ask me where I'm going when I hop into a three-wheeler in Colombo. To the women at the fruit stands on the side of the road. To the man who sells me kottu roti.

"Next year will you come with your husband."

My great aunt Ratna says this without a question mark at the end.

We are sitting in her dining room. I am spooning rice and curry into my mouth with my fingers, hoping I'm doing it right. Hoping I'm doing it right, even though I've been eating rice and curry with my fingers for my whole life. Hoping I'm doing it right even though I know how to make rice and curry and can probably guess what is in most of these dishes. Turmeric, garlic, cumin, chili seed in that one. Not enough salt in this one. She must have put coconut powder into this one—is that how you get the sauce so thick? I'll ask her.

"Auntie, is there coconut powder in this?"

"Eh?"

"Did you use coconut powder? With the potatoes. I want to know so I can try and make it at home."

"You cook?" She seems genuinely shocked.

"Yeah, I love cooking." I say, carefully pulling dahl and rice across my plate toward the lady's fingers. I push my own fingers into the tapered greens, my nails slipping in their slimy innards. I do not know why I'm trying to make this into a perfect ball. Dhal and rice bits are slipping up past my knuckles.

"So, next time you'll bring your husband, yes?"

Ratna is unfazed by my attempted culinary evasion or the neuroses affecting my plate skills.

I laugh politely. "I don't know, Auntie. I like travelling on my own."

This is my third trip to Sri Lanka. My third time meeting my grandmother's sisters. There are only two left: Sister Mary Lucy, a retired nun, and Ratna, mother of eight and grandmother of at least four. At eighty-nine and eighty-five, my time with them is limited and precious, especially considering I only met them three years ago.

This is my third trip to see them but my first time truly experiencing the fullness of what it means to have a South Asian auntie. I grew up with white aunts, my mother's sisters. All of my father's family was somewhere on the other side of the equator, and only one of them had married into the same colour. My father's eldest brother's wife was Gujarati. Much to my grandmother's ire and never earning her forgiveness, there were no nice Tamil girls who would fill the role of the daughter she never had. So I had no brown aunties, and when it came to the post-wedding/funeral/family reunion/birthday debrief with my young, brown female friends, the bonding experience was one I could only peripherally enjoy. Despite the irritation, there was always laughter and fondness underlying these stories and a closeness I wanted with women I wish I knew.

"Come, come, there must be some boy at home."

"Nope. No boy."

I try not to emphasize the word. Uncertain of myself, I slink back in the closet for the first time in ten years. Am I safe?

"There must be one she's not telling us," my Auntie Lucy pipes up. She is watching the cricket match that's playing in the background. India versus Australia. India is winning.

"Dada is not finding anyone for you?"

"No, he's not really involved in the process."

"Mumma then. You must call Mumma, and I will talk to her, and we will see about this. I am sure they have someone for you."

My parents had never expressed any particular needs or wants over my romantic life or my uterine destiny. Any time I had mentioned even the vaguest fantasies about procreating, my mother's instant reply was always, "Don't have children. They ruin your life."

"Aw, thanks, Mom."

"Not you—you and Sacha are perfect. But children are far too much work, and you'll never have your own life again. Don't touch the walls!"

She runs to get a rag.

My father says I should do whatever makes me happy. Babies love him, and sometimes I think it would be nice for him to be a grandpa. But not at the expense of me having to be a mother.

"How old are you?" Ratna asks.

"Guess."

"Twenty-two," offers Sister Lucy.

"Twenty," says Ratna.

"I'm twenty-nine."

Ratna's eyebrows shoot up. "Oh dear, well you're still young." She sounds doubtful. "But soon you will have to get married."

Ratna is the youngest daughter in a family of seven siblings, and her birth ended her mother's life. Lucy thinks she never recovered from that moment. "That's why she thinks no one cares enough about her. But her children take such good care of her. Tell me, what is there for her to worry?"

After their mother died giving birth to her final child, the four older girls were sent to a convent school. Their grandmother had ten children of her own, some as young as her grandchildren. "One day, Akka did not come to school, and they asked us, 'Where is she? Where is Saras? We didn't know.' That is when Granny told us she was married. The nuns were very upset. 'She was such a smart girl. Why did you marry her?' But Granny said, 'These children have no one, their mother is dead, there is only me, and if something happens to me, they will have no one, these girls.'" So Saraswathy, goddess of knowledge, the eldest at fifteen, already mother to her own six siblings, was married to Ratnarajah, thirty-two.

"She didn't even say goodbye to you?"

"No, Granny only told us later."

My grandmother died during a northeastern winter. Already shuffled between continents and competing brothers like an unwanted heirloom. Regifted until she was too shabby to ship. She died of Parkinson's in a room with no window in my uncle's Virginia duplex.

"Her five jewels," Aunt Lucy said, laughing her dry laugh. Tharmarajah, Sivarajah, Kularajah, Devarajah, Premarajah. She counts off my father and his brothers on her fingers. She does this often. "Akka had five sons.

Tharmarajah, Sivarajah, Kularajah, Devarajah, Premarajah." I asked her once, "Why all this rajah?" She said, "They are my five kings! My five stars."

I didn't know that version of my grandmother. Lucy's version.

Their father was a drunk. He ran all the way to Malaysia to drink. He died there. They do not know when. Then Saraswathy went to live there with a functioning alcoholic for sixty years. Marriage on this side of the family seems to drive the men to drink and the women to prayer. Even the next generation followed in their footsteps. Some of the women stopped praying to divorce instead. Or die. Or wait till the men died. My father will not drink. He even hates it when my mom has a glass of wine. "It's a toxin," he says. "It kills your brain cells."

"There might be someone you don't know about yet," Auntie Lucy says.

"Maybe."

"There must be someone thinking of you that you don't know," she insists.

Before Sister Mary Lucy was Sister Mary Lucy, she was Padmalakshmi. The third child. "They always said I was the lucky girl because two boys were born after me." She says this proudly.

She has been a nun for over sixty years. Twenty of those years were spent in Madagascar, where she contracted cerebral malaria. The brain fever resulted in short-term memory loss. She tells me the same stories over and over. I don't know whether I should pretend to be hearing them for the first time, but I do anyway. Sometimes there is a new detail.

"Granny was very angry that I wanted to enter. She said, 'What is it that I have not given you that you want to leave the world?' I wanted to see the world, though, not leave it. And I wanted to help children—orphans like us."

"Did you ever want your own children, Auntie? Were you ever in love?"

"What love do I need but the love of God? No, no."

Then the fifth time I hear the story: "Before I entered, the mother superior came to me. She said, 'Before you decide, you must read these letters.' I said, 'What letters? I have never seen any letters.'"

"Letters from boys, Auntie?"

"All those boys! They had come for me, and she had hidden them. I told her, 'I don't need to see them. You can burn them.'"

"You didn't keep any of them?"

"I had no need to see them. I had chosen my path."

They both ask if I am Catholic. No. Muslim? No. Hindu then. No. Do I believe in anything?

Let's talk about marriage again!

"Next year you will come with your husband," says Ratna.

"Yes, Auntie."

SWIMMING LESSONS

I wear a bikini under my dress

I pull the fabric up

and up

and up

Not all the way

Brown women stumble laughing into the waves

Bright lenghas stained dark from the heavy salt water

The weight of the fabric pulling away from collarbones

Sucking close to their bodies

Dupattas sparkle and float gently in the rhythm of the tide

I learned how to swim in a chlorine pool

Encased in spandex

My teenage instructor

Long limbs and bright hair shining

Through the membrane of the water's surface

The edge of the pool is slippery

She is unreachable

Her directions bounce off the concrete

Hold your breath

Five, five, five, five

Four, four, four, four

Three, three, three, three

Two, two, two, two

One, one, one, one

I want to dive into the ocean with them
These chattering women
I want to shed this cloth and my skin
I pull my dress down around my ankles
And dig my feet into the sand

Adapted from a talk given at EMMA Talks, Vancouver, BC, 2018:
http://emmatalks.org/video/anoushka-ratnarajah/

In the Shadow of Bluebeard's Castle

Margret Killjoy

There's this fairy tale; maybe you've heard it before: Bluebeard's Castle. It's sort of a feminist parable, in the old-school way where a lot of traditional folklore is basically saying, "Hey women, don't trust men—they will murder you."

Far too often, accountability processes and attempts at restorative justice in radical communities empower abusers and assaulters. Whenever I think about that, I think about Bluebeard's Castle. Here's the short version:

There's this rich dude named Bluebeard. He lives in a castle. He marries this young village woman and brings her to the castle. She's the protagonist, inasmuch as fairy tales have protagonists. Hurray! Dream come true! She gets to live in a castle and not worry about her material conditions!

He's like, "Hey babe, you can go anywhere you want in the castle. It's your home now. Except don't go into my man cave. Man cave is strictly off limits. Anyway, here are the keys to every single room, including the one you're not allowed to go into. I'm gonna go on a work trip or some shit. Have fun. Don't go into my man cave."

You'll be shocked to know that curiosity gets the better of our young heroine, and she goes into his forbidden room of forbidden-ness. Inside, she finds the mutilated, murdered bodies of all his ex-wives. He comes home and is gonna kill her as punishment for having betrayed his trust by going into his man cave. Her brothers show up in the nick of time and kill Bluebeard instead.

The end.

There are some feminist retellings of Bluebeard's Castle floating around, involving her rescuing herself, or her mom shows up and saves her, or whatever, instead of her brothers, or whatever. I'm going to propose a more cynical telling, a half-feminist one—the modern man's Bluebeard's Castle, if you will.

In this retelling, Bluebeard has agreed to be upfront about his past. He's being accountable. As our young, newlywed bride approaches his castle, she sees corpses on display—imagine something gruesome so I don't have to type it out.

"So, before you move in," he says, even though they've already done the marriage ceremony in town, and it's kinda too late to back out now, "there's something you should know about me. See all these dead bodies? They're my ex-wives. I killed all of them." Then he turns to her with an earnest look in his beautiful eyes. "I've learned a lot since then. I'm being accountable."

"Don't worry," the newlywed bride says—maybe she's still in the throes of infatuation, or maybe she's taking a calculated risk based on the living standards and life expectancy available to her if she doesn't marry a rich man—"I know you'd never murder *me*."

"I'm so glad I can trust you to know this about me," Bluebeard says.

Then they move into the castle and either live happily ever after or he murders her.

Most attempts to hold sexual assaulters and abusers accountable, that I've witnessed, are not revolutionary. I don't mean *revolutionary* in the grand class-struggle sense. I mean it in the overthrowing-of-an-existing-norm sense. Most attempts at accountability stop as soon as the status quo is restored and everyone (except, often, the survivor) is comfortable enough. As we've learned from history, half-revolutions get you killed.

Half-revolutions leave the ruling class as they are. Worse, they give the ruling class new tools with which to suppress dissent. In the same way that capitalist democracy makes us feel culpable in our own oppression by pretending to give us access to state power. Half-feminism leaves abusers in our midst, still controlling us, while making the survivors look more culpable for their own mistreatment.

In the half-feminist Bluebeard, it's easier to blame the new bride for either her own murder—or her life lived in fear of it—after all, she knew what she was getting into; he was honest with her.

This is not to say we shouldn't hold ourselves and others accountable for actions. Instead, it's to say we don't go far enough in the process. We don't trust ourselves and one another enough to take meaningful action against people or to demand real change from them. We stop halfway.

Those of us who desire a society without prisons, courts and all the apparatus of state-led "justice" have a particularly interesting path to navigate as we consider solutions to these problems. But our choice is not between a soft-handed version of restorative justice or a heavy-handed justice system based on mass incarceration.

I've been part of a number of anarchist and activist communities, mostly throughout the United States. I've witnessed and assisted many attempts to hold perpetrators of sexual assault accountable to their communities. There are a few patterns that seem to crop up every time. One of the most pervasive and perhaps the most harmful is a mimicking of legal structure and an insistence on following the "letter" of accountability agreements rather than the "spirit" of them.

We're so heavily indoctrinated into believing in legal systems that we bring legalistic language and solutions to our practices of restorative-justice. A legal system has laws—that is, it has exact and codified rules. Once put into place, those laws are hard or impossible to change. That's the entire basis of a legal system. A legal system has no place in healthy restorative practice.

When you make laws, you make lawyers. When you write down rules, you challenge people to find loopholes in those rules instead of solutions to the problems those rules were written to address. Worse, when you insist upon a specific, legalistic accountability practice, you force survivors, or their supporters, to write down the steps of it. And you refuse to acknowledge that their desires and needs, let alone their understanding of the situation, might change over time. It took me months to accept that I'd been raped, and years to internalize how I felt about that. There's no way I could have constructed a meaningful restorative practice on a quick timeline. Since I didn't yet understand what happened to me or how best to heal from it, I couldn't even have been of much use to any group of people who were attempting to work on my behalf.

Legalistic feminism is half-feminism. The creation of laws will never be more than a half-revolution.

A revolutionary feminist retelling of Bluebeard's Castle involves all the villagers who live in that castle's shadow, not just the brothers, and it involves pitchforks and torches, and its last line might be "dashed upon the rocks, left to be eaten by birds and by the sea."

I use the serial murder of women by a misogynist as a hyperbolic example. While as much as it is pleasant to dwell on the idea of throwing abusers off freeway overpasses into traffic, that might not always be the solution we're looking for. In fact, there is no single solution, and the search for one is a distraction.

I do know that there are many solutions that come up time and time again that are not solutions at all. Asking an assaulter to disclose their past, in private, to new partners will never be enough. Without community support, most of us would walk past any number of corpses for the chance to live safe in a castle.

We should be talking about picket lines in front of the gatehouse. We should be talking about how to dismantle the castle walls, stone by stone, or how to open its doors to collective living.

Even those of us who consider ourselves radicals can get so caught up in the surface of problems that we never address the problems at their roots. To stretch our metaphor to its furthest reaches: we're so concerned about Bluebeard's property rights that we never consider what life without him living in that castle might look like. Or to speak in specifics, far too often, we take it for granted even in radical communities, that the abusers have a right to continue to access our spaces, that they have a right to continue to accrue social capital. Through the guise of accountability, they even have a new revenue stream of social capital.

I believe in restorative justice. I've seen it work. I've also seen survivors driven from communities over and over again. That ostracizing of survivors is rarely explicit. Everyone says, "I believe survivors." Everyone says, "The survivor's needs are the focus of accountability." But so often, at their heart, accountability processes assume the goal of reconciliation. They want to make sure the abuser is able to continue to access the community and are just looking for ways to make that possible.

Sometimes, maybe most of the time, it will never be possible.

I don't believe it is fair, radical, or effective to expect survivors or their immediate supporters to share community with their rapists and abusers. It's important for us—and certainly for abusers—to understand that certain actions have permanent consequences: "Never initiate conversation with me ever again" is a completely reasonable request in some circumstances.

What is a genuinely accountable and contrite Bluebeard to do? I'm afraid of generalizing by using this metaphor, but I'll try anyway: Bluebeard should give up his castle, probably to the families of those he's harmed. He should move somewhere else, to another community that knows what he has done and is dedicated to helping hold him accountable in a place where none of his victims or their loved ones will ever need to fear him or see him again.

It's easier for me to be certain about what I perceive as problems: that disclosure alone is almost worthless; that our focus on reconciliation does little to mitigate ongoing damage to survivors. It's far harder for me to be certain about the solutions I offer.

What I know is that we don't want honest oppressors; we want no one in a position of power from which to oppress us. We want to never live in the shadow of the castle again.

....

This essay is slightly adapted from a blogpost:
http://birdsbeforethestorm.net/2018/04/in-the-shadow-of-bluebeards-castle/

Where are the Gears?
Thoughts on Resisting the (Neoliberal, Networked) Machine

Astra Taylor

In 1964, Mario Savio, a young graduate student at the University of California, Berkeley, gave a speech that would come to symbolize the 1960s and the decade's spirit of youthful revolt. Students recently active in the civil rights movement wanted to pamphlet and table political causes on school property. When they were denied that right, the Free Speech Movement took off.[1] In part, Savio said,

> There's a time when the operation of the machine becomes so odious, makes you so sick at heart that you can't take part! You can't even passively take part! And you've got to put your bodies upon the gears and upon the wheels, upon the levers, upon all the apparatus—and you've got to make it stop! And you've got to indicate to the people who run it, to the people who own it, that unless you're free the machine will be prevented from working at all!

Today Savio's speech still resonates: the operation of the machine is, indeed, odious, and we must stop it. How do we shut it down—or better yet, how do we remake the machine into something more equitable and just? These are questions that Savio and his comrades weren't able to answer, even as they racked up some concrete victories.

In a sense, the Free Speech Movement was victorious. The students won both the right to pamphlet on university property and other concessions from the administration. And the events have been memorialized to the max and fully incorporated into Berkeley's brand. Today, there's an official Free Speech Café on campus, where students gossip and study surrounded by black-and-white photos of those heady days. The steps at Sproul Plaza are even named for Mario Savio and can be reserved by groups that want to pontificate.

There was, however, another California protest movement that was far more successful, though less well known. It protested property taxes and paved the way for tax revolts nationwide, laying the groundwork for Ronald Reagan, the conservative backlash of the 1980s, the Tea Party, and even the rise of Donald Trump.

Forty years ago, on June 6, 1978, that grassroots campaign won a huge victory which eventually transformed this country's economic bedrock. But instead of studying *their* efforts, and learning from *their* success, the campus protests from the previous decade remain far better known. Though Savio and his fellow student protesters may have been on the right side of history, it was their less visible conservative counterparts who more successfully remade American political life according to their designs.

In the early sixties, dramatic images of young people standing up both to censorship and Berkeley's campus police captured the imagination of the Baby Boom generation and the media's attention. The rebellion also captivated the man who was then a candidate for Governor of California, Ronald Reagan.

Reagan tapped a deep well of anti-student sentiments, vowing to "clean up the mess at Berkeley"—his other main campaign promise was to send the "welfare bums back to work." He painted the protesters as unpatriotic intellectual snobs and spoiled brats. Other factors played into Reagan's success, of course, but the University of California at Berkeley provided a useful political foil: a hotbed of sexual, social, generational, and even communist deviance that he could make his name condemning and cracking down on. He then sowed the seeds for our current obsession with "liberal permissiveness." As governor, Reagan eventually got rid of the man Mario Savio called that "well-meaning liberal," Berkeley President Clark Kerr, who was canned for being too "soft" on the protesters.[2]

Writing in *Dissent*, Mike Konczal and Aaron Bady argue that "It's important to remember this chapter in California history because it . . . signaled the beginning of the end of public higher education in the United States as we'd known it."[3]

Reagan's rhetoric was not empty. A few years after the Free Speech Movement, when more protests took place, he called in the National Guard to crush those protests, which it did with unprecedented severity. More importantly, to punish the allegedly coddled students, he cut state funding to higher education and laid the foundations for a shift to a tuition-based funding model at state schools which had, until that point, minus some nominal fees, been free. Konczal and Bady write:

> [Reagan] was only able to do this because he had already successfully shifted the political debate over the meaning and purpose of public higher education in America. The first "bums" he threw off welfare were California university students. Instead of seeing the education of the state's youth as a patriotic duty and a vital weapon in the Cold War, he cast universities as a problem in and of themselves—both an expensive welfare program and dangerously close to socialism. He even argued for the importance of tuition-based funding by suggesting that if students had to pay, they'd value their education too much to protest.

Channeling public antipathy toward the young rebels, Reagan attacked state-funded universities and advanced the cause of privatization. Anticipating a strategy successfully employed by the reality-tv-launched plutocrat Donald Trump, a branded-content-and-movie-star-turned-politician burnished his reputation by pointing an accusatory finger at the so-called "cultural elite."

In retrospect, it's clear that Savio's speech foreshadowed some of the core problems plaguing universities today: the corporatization of higher education and the fact that neoliberalism forces us to think of ourselves in what are essentially corporate terms: as small individual firms, seeking a return on what we've paid or borrowed to get a college degree. Reagan boosted these trends by cutting education funding and instituting tuition as part of his campaign against the Free Speech Movement.

Reagan, however, didn't despise every protest he encountered. Thirteen years after the Free Speech Movement, a tax revolt erupted in Southern California. Only instead of helping him win the lowly Governorship, this movement helped him win the White House.

Much like the Tea Party, which it presaged, the tax revolt was a movement of older people. It was not a purely right-wing movement, at first—instead, it appealed to people at both ends of the political spectrum.

Out-of-control inflation had given homeowners, especially elderly folks on fixed incomes, legitimate financial grievances, and those folks needed relief. These were people who bought houses years or decades ago when they were cheap and lived in their homes since. But property taxes, which had ballooned as prices rose, meant threatening some vulnerable residents with eviction.

This genuine problem provided a man named Howard Jarvis with the opportunity he had been looking for.

Jarvis was fiercely antigovernment and had attempted to organize against the federal income tax in the past but hadn't made much headway. A successful businessman who owned newspapers and real estate, Jarvis was driven by a profoundly right-wing political ideology: he vigorously opposed many of the things taxes paid for—schools, parks, libraries, and garbage collection.

"The most important thing in this country is not the school system, nor the police department, nor the fire department," Jarvis said. "The right to preserve, the right to have property in this country, the right to have a home in this country—that's important."

What Jarvis did, brilliantly, was yoke his extremely conservative anti-state ideology, which opposed taxation and government generally, to the highly particular, concrete problems faced by people in his community. As a tireless organizer, he gathered the needed signatures to get a ballot initiative on the agenda, which meant it could be voted on by the citizens of California directly and bypass the legislative process, where it likely would have stalled. On June 6, 1978, Proposition 13, formally the People's Initiative to Limit Property Taxation, passed in a landslide, and property taxes were radically cut.

Homeowners received the tax relief they sought, but many experts question whether Californians understood what they were voting for. Proposition 13 seemed simple but actually wasn't. Jarvis not only lowered property taxes to reasonable levels, he decimated them. The initiative rolled back property assessments and froze them at 1975 levels; the values could then be raised by only two percent a year, while properties could only be reassessed at times of sale or transfer, when they would be taxed at a flat one percent of the new value. This, of course, choked state revenue, disappearing billions of dollars.

This was bad enough, but there were other details few voters paid close attention to:

- Proposition 13 applied to corporate and rental properties, not just primary residences: Homes change hands more frequently than businesses, getting re-assessed every time. Famously, Disney Land's property taxes are based on 1978 assessments; and
- Proposition 13 had a provision prohibiting any local or state government body from raising new taxes without a two-thirds vote of the governing body, making it virtually impossible to ever repeal.

Jarvis was nothing if not savvy. He understood the system he was trying to transform and how he wanted to change it, including how to stop future generations from changing his law.

He also who knew his audience and how to pander to them. He might have been an old curmudgeon, but the Proposition 13 tax revolt was a protest born of a changing media era and was highly theatrical.

Jarvis partly modelled his "everyman" persona on the star character of the hit film *Network*—he even named his popular book *I'm Mad As Hell* in homage to his cinematic hero who breaks with the script on national television to declare "I'm mad as hell, and I'm not going to take this anymore."

And so, what we have here is the ultimate all-American movement: a movement spearheaded by a businessman inspired by a Hollywood film that appealed to the movie actor aspiring to the presidency.

When Proposition 13 passed, Jarvis declared it "a victory against money, the politicians, the government." "Government simply must be limited," he went on. "Excessive taxation leads to either bankruptcy or dictatorship." (In 2015, when I met with some of Jarvis's core collaborators at their office in Sacramento, they compared their efforts to those of Robin Hood—a figure who, in their telling, was not robbing the rich to give to the poor but courageously resisting overzealous tax collectors). Reagan, sensing opportunity, agreed. He saw the resolution as a rebellion against "costly, overpowering government" and urged other Republicans to recognize its significance and utility.

Here, at last, was a way to get regular Americans—who weren't particularly skeptical of government at that point—to join a movement that imagined government as the enemy. Working- and middle-class communities were justifiably angry that they were bearing the brunt of inflation by paying out-of-control and erratically assessed property taxes. That anger was used to pry open the door to nationwide contempt for taxes in general—contempt that ultimately benefited wealthy citizens and large corporations, not average homeowners.

Soon, tax-limiting initiatives began spreading state to state across the nation, and Reagan made the shrewd decision to get on board. According to scholars, Proposition 13 set the stage for his conservative revolution. In their book *Chain Reaction: The Impact of Race, Rights, and Taxes on American Politics*, Mary and Thomas Edsall call the tax revolt "a major turning point," a campaign and set of policies that "provided conservatism with a powerful internal coherence, shaping an anti-government ethic and firmly establishing new grounds for the disaffection of white working- and middle-class voters from their Democratic roots." The electorate was divided between "taxpayers" and "tax recipients," a wedge that fell along predictable racial lines.

Indeed, it's hard to imagine today, but before the Proposition 13 movement and Reagan's presidential campaign, tax cuts were simply not the fundamental issue they are today. Isaac Martin, author of *The Permanent Tax Revolt* and *Rich People's Movements*, argues that it was not so much that people's attitudes toward taxes changed but rather that the approach of political parties did—taxes now seen as something politicians were either for or against.

When we talk about neoliberalism, or whatever we want to call our current economic reality, we often think of it as a top-down affair driven by Austrian and Chicago School economists, politicians, CEOs, and technocrats—and in fundamental respects, it once was. But these tax revolts are an important part of the story, specifically the part where neoliberalism appealed, on some level, to everyday people—and it still does. As these conservative, antitaxation, anti-state policies caught on, they provided the business community with invaluable cover.

Many well-funded corporate groups have done their part to push tax cuts as a major political issue, and stoking white racial resentment and welfare chauvinism (based on the idea that the state should only support "deserving" populations, who are typically presented as white and middle and upper class, while poor and racialized groups are portrayed as "undeserving" of support) have been central to their approach. But without the movement of angry California homeowners, they may not have known how to frame their positions in a way that could at least *plausibly* appear palatable, or even popular.

In this respect it was a key moment of right-wing show-business politics we see today; a toxic combination of populist electioneering and plutocratic governance taken to a whole new level by our current president.

The Free Speech Movement and the Proposition 13 tax revolt aren't usually discussed in the same breath. But they should be.

The Free Speech Movement shaped a common image of resistance and cemented the idea of the university student as an agent of change. It was iconic—hipster youth shaking fists at the authorities, playing guitar, and standing on police cars look cool.

Looking back, the Berkeley protests played a role in changing the way we understand political resistance. Even if you've never heard of it, the Free Speech movement shaped public perceptions of activism, helping cement the image of young people, especially students, as preeminent agents of political change.

This was the period—the 1960s—when our society, especially the political left, seized on the idea that young people had a special role to play in political movements and were, in some cases, the revolutionary vanguard par excellence. (In his famous "Letter to the New Left" C. Wright Mills made the case that youth had replaced the working class as the "historic agency"; Theodore Roszak, who was a popularize of the term *counterculture*, called this shift the "adolescentization of dissent.")

The myth of youthful activism or political radicalism always struck me as a bit strange, since, in reality, not all young people are activists, progressive, or left wing—and they certainly were not in the sixties. But given then shifting demographics, changing social mores, and the draft and the war in Vietnam, this perception made more sense at the time. Today, though, the myth's shortcomings are more apparent. There's a standard assumption that being an activist is just a phase, a kind of youthful folly one grows out of; the emphasis on youth fosters counterproductive generational divisions and resentments. Also, while student activism is undeniably vital, it can occasionally eclipse other models of collective action.

The Right wing, meanwhile, doesn't fetishize youth in the same way. Theda Skocpol's *The Tea Party and the Remaking of Republican Conservatism* describes a movement proud to be a movement of older people dedicated to spending their golden years fighting to "take their country back." These individuals are established in communities, have retirement income, and have lots of time on their hands—all useful attributes if you want to effectively push for social and political change.

The tax revolters, then, were anything but iconic or hip. But they were effective, finding the gears and the levers they needed and bringing them to a halt.

The gears were both political and economic. First, they understood the machinations of government. They attracted the needed signatures to put Proposition 13 on the ballot and then locked in their victory by insisting on the requirement of a supermajority vote to impose new taxes, effectively eliminating the possibility that the measure would be undone—a stroke of genius. Second, they had a highly politicized vision of taxation and of spending. And that vision has had a tremendous impact on both California and the nation.

It's worth lingering on the consequences of Proposition 13. Michael Stewart Foley's writes in *Front Porch Politics:*

> In Proposition 13's aftermath, local government saw more than $6 billion in funding evaporate. The state moved to use its surplus to offset the losses, but even so, municipalities cut services and laid people off. San Francisco closed twenty-six schools, laid off a thousand teachers, and doubled the mass transit fare to fifty cents. Officials made wholesale cuts to state mental health and developmentally disabled programs, dumping patients into "rooming houses and inadequate nursing homes." Some cities lost their school bus systems and others saw summer school and arts, music, and sports programming cut . . . . [W]hereas the state's schools had been "among the most generously funded in the nation," they were now "in the bottom quarter among the states in virtually every major indicator—in their physical condition, in public funding, in test scores." Universities that had once been tuition free became expensive, and the state's infrastructure—the freeway system that had once been the envy of the nation—was "now rated among the most dilapidated road networks in the country." In the meantime, the big winners were the big corporations and commercial property owners: Pacific Telephone saved $130 million; Pacific Gas & Electric, over $90 million; Standard Oil, $13 million in Contra Costa County alone.

If that's not success, I don't know what is.

Proof of Howard Jarvis's victory abounds. Consider, for example, what should have been a scandal but wasn't. While on the campaign trail, Trump was able to take pride in the fact that he had paid minimal taxes over the years to the very government he was campaigning to take the helm of. "That makes me smart," he said in his first debate with Hillary Clinton. Besides, he said later, any tax paid "would be squandered, too, believe me." Jarvis would have cheered.

A generation ago the tax revolters found the gears. Now we on the Left need to do the same.

Taxes are a brilliant lever for conservatives "made sick at heart" by the operation of the state—specifically, the parts that regulate corporations, set labor standards, provide healthcare to people, educate kids whose parents don't have money to pay for private tutors, and protect the environment—to not just make it grind it to a halt, but to completely transform its functioning. *Starve the beast; drown it in a bathtub*—these are the conservatives' slogans. The wealthy have been on a long and extremely successful tax revolt for at least the last four decades, but arguably much longer.

Proposition 13 can only be understood in a broader context of right-wing retrenchment and reaction. Some see the law's passage as a response to a set of California Supreme Court decisions requiring property taxes to be redistributed to poor areas. When I interviewed political theorist Wendy Brown for my 2018 documentary, *What Is Democracy?* she told me Proposition 13 was the "first big retort that you get in the twentieth century in America to the idea essentially of redistribution for public goods and for the sake of equality of opportunity and educating us in common." Other scholars have noted that these events unfolded in California right as the Black Panthers were making their bid for municipal power in Oakland.

In retrospect, the chain of events leading from Southern California to the White House might seem like fait accompli. But the Proposition 13 movement began humbly, when a handful of cranky seniors burnt their tax assessment notices on the Capitol steps. What if the legitimate fears of people over ballooning housing costs had been addressed in another way? As Brown noted when we met, more constructive responses to such grievances were (and still are) possible:

> We could have responded to people who lived in houses who had fixed incomes by having different tax rates for people with fixed incomes. We could have responded to skyrocketing housing prices with anti-speculation laws. We could have responded to skyrocketing housing prices by capping the values of property. Instead of capping property taxes we could have capped housing price increases.

Unfortunately, an alternative set of solutions, based on democratizing and decommodifying housing, was never articulated. The resurgent Right, not the Left, stepped in and spoke to people's anxieties.

It is a mistake we shouldn't repeat, even if our task is not as straightforward as lambasting taxes. The Left can't engage in such easy, revenue-withholding nihilism, since we want to build a better world not just tear down social services. Our complex task is made more difficult by the fact that what are arguably the most crucial gears for progressives, labor unions, are under relentless attack and face all kinds of legal restrictions. At the same time, decades of antitax and antiwelfare organizing on the part of business elites means that many Americans, though by no means all, are reluctant recognize that public goods and regulation—like social housing and anti-speculation laws—could be part of the solution to what ails them.

Given the very real challenges we face, we need to think creatively. But these are dilemmas we need to tackle head on, not shy away from.

As Martin Luther King argued in his prescient 1968 book *Where Do We Go from Here: Chaos or Community?* social and economic progress has stalled out in part because the changes we aim to make require substantial resources. "The practical cost of change for the nation up to this point has been cheap," King writes. "There are no expenses, and no taxes are required, for Negroes to share lunch counters, libraries, parks, hotels, and other facilities with whites . . . . Jobs are harder and costlier to create than voting rolls. The eradication of slums housing millions is complex far beyond integrating buses and lunch counters." The things we are fighting for today—whether we are talking about closing prisons in favor of restorative-justice programs, instituting public healthcare, eliminating student debt and providing universal education, and combating climate change and building new green infrastructure—demand investment and redistribution. They also mean a loss of revenue for the capitalist class, which partly explains why these fights are so difficult to win. "The real cost lies ahead," King warned. What's more, building "power for poor people" will require difficult, unglamorous work.

Mass demonstrations will not be enough. They must be supplemented by a continuing job of organization. To produce change, people must be organized into units of power. These units may be political, as in the case of voters' leagues and political parties; they may be economic, as in the case of groups of tenants who join forces to form a union, or groups of the unemployed and underemployed who organize to get better wages. This task is tedious, as it lacks the drama of demonstrations, but it is necessary to produce meaningful results.

In the United States after Trump's election, people rallied around being "ungovernable," an evocative, appealing idea. But the thing is, I want the Left to actually govern someday, to not just be ungovernable. I don't want to see people throwing sand or having their bodies ground up into dust by the gears of the machine. I want intelligent, kind-hearted, future-oriented people to remake the machine, to change its gears, and run it democratically for once.

With this aim in mind, fifty years from now, my wish is to have played a small part in some obscure group, one remembered not for rousing speeches or dramatic confrontations, but for helping to develop new effective modes of resistance and ways of remaking the state so it serves human ends. A group not remembered for being iconic or cool but for having the acuity to find the levers of power, the good sense to strategize about how to grab them, and the stamina for the tedium required to actually pull off such a plan. The alternative is to leave the machine to run as it is—to run over our communities, our environment, and our future.

....

This is an adaptation of the EMMA Talk given May 2017, Vancouver, BC: http://emmatalks.org/video/astra-taylor/

1. Watch the full speech here, https://www.youtube.com/watch?v=tcx9BJRadfw

2, 3. https://www.dissentmagazine.org/article/from-master-plan-to-no-plan-the -slow-death-of-public-higher-education

CHAPTER FIVE

Soaring

Being heard
We rise
sharing our songs
We rise together.

Above the clouds
into the moonlight
We fly
imagining anew
Thriving
me, you, us.
joyfully

   We love

—carla bergman

Everything Inside of Us

Tasnim Nathoo

A few years ago, I read an essay about the history of carrots. Before the appearance of the modern orange carrot we know today, the pale and unremarkable looking parsnip was the darling of the European kitchen. Who knew? Yes, indeed, the starchy and sweet parsnip was prized for its versatility. But then came the boldly coloured orange carrot. And the magnificently starchy potato. And the sweet beet. And that was it for the parsnip. Poor parsnip. This story apparently was still in the back of my mind the next time I went to the grocery store because I then proceeded to buy a bag of parsnips. And a couple of turnips. And a rutabaga. And a few other root vegetables that I felt were no longer getting enough credit or limelight in a world of vibrant carrots and glorious beets. When I got home, my room-mate looked at the kitchen counter and said, "You're such a social worker! You even care about the stigmatized vegetables"—a plausible interpretation of my interest in the plight of unfashionable vegetables.

Championing the wonders of root vegetables is a pretty exciting but minor part of my life. I seem to spend an increasing amount of time doing my best to provide people with the tools they need to heal themselves. At first, people really seemed to resist this idea. "What? I can heal myself? No way. I'm here because I want *you* to heal me—or another expert. Maybe there's some kind of pill? Algae or something with too many syllables to pronounce?" A disbelief in our innate ability to heal seems a consequence

The bold carrot   The glorious beet   The unfashionable parsnip

of modern life—perhaps because we have benefited in so many ways from experts, impenetrable science, and marvellous medical discoveries, like antibiotics and anesthesia.

Everything we need to heal is inside of us. There, I said it. When I first heard this idea, I was floored. It was one of the most radical things I had ever heard. But with gentle prodding, encouragement from some wonderful teachers, and regular and frequent reminders from folks I was privileged to work with, I came around.

Here's an example that helped to convince me. If we cut our finger while making something scrumptious in the kitchen, our finger heals itself. (There are exceptions, of course, but for the purposes of this example, let us not go there). If things are a little messier, we might apply a bandage of some kind for a few days—and there are now quite a few fashionable options available. But really, it is our finger that does the healing—the colourful bandage only provides support and protection during this process. If things are grimmer, we might head to a clinic or hospital for stitches. But the stitches are mostly just holding things together until our finger figures out how to fix things up. Sometimes, things do not go back to how they were before the kitchen upset—we might get a scar or forever be super aware of our fingers near sharp knives. But we do heal, and we can continue to live full lives, inside and outside the kitchen.

I am in no way minimizing the awesomeness of modern medicine. I am pro—modern medicine. I think it is wonderful. If you have a heart attack or something like that, please, call emergency services or go directly to your local hospital. But I think we're all aware that there are many things modern medicine cannot fix or struggles to fix. Many of us have found ourselves "medical orphans" with hurts that cannot be diagnosed or, if diagnosed, there are no easy solutions or treatments. I think this is especially true when talking about healing from individual and collective experiences of trauma.

Did you know *trauma* is a Greek word meaning "wound"? Interestingly, it has been associated with non-physical wounds for quite some time. The Greek historian Herodotus, way back in 490 BCE, described an Athenian solider in the Battle of Marathon who went blind after witnessing a fellow soldier's death. The soldier did not have a physical wound yet was deeply affected by what he saw. He experienced a *psychic wound* or a *soul wound*, something invisible but no less real than other kinds of war injuries.

Many of us are scared to talk about trauma. We minimize it, lock it up, or ignore it. I think it's because we've picked up the idea that healing from trauma is really hard, hopeless, or requires ten years of therapy. When I started working in the mental health and substance use field, I was shocked no one wanted to talk about trauma, even though it was an elephant in almost every room we entered. Things are starting to change, but I think we still believe in trauma as a Pandora's box. '*Do Not Open: You will unleash misery and make things worse.*' (For the record, scholars actually think Pandora opened up a large storage jar and this somehow was mistranslated as '*box*'.) I think we have forgotten our innate ability to heal. We trust we can heal physical injuries, if occasionally needing marvellous medical interventions. So why not our invisible wounds?

What supports and protects us while we heal from trauma in the way bandages and stitches do for our physical wounds? The answer will be different for different folks in different places, of course. But some of the things that seem to be common to the stories of many of the people I have worked with include:

- Spiritual practices that allow us to find answers to questions like: *Who am I? What is my purpose? Where do I belong? Do I need to forgive?* For some people, spirituality means rediscovering or more deeply investigating their faith or cultural traditions. For others, spirituality might mean reading about philosophy, surfing, or acts of service.
- Activism in which we can bring balance to the world through collective action and work to heal the root causes of our wounds.
- Learning to listen to ourselves. Many people talk about deep inner listening or finding a sense of quiet, or stillness and how this helps to make them whole again. People seem to find all sorts of ways to do this. Meditation, mindfulness, contemplation, prayer, art making, and time in nature are time-honoured paths. It's not really about thinking and reflecting, just being aware. And sometimes, if needed, wonderful ideas about what we need to heal will bubble up.
- Sleep, movement, nourishing food, and good people. These things usually make us feel a little better right away and they make it so much easier for our bodies to do their healing thing.

There is an idea in many healing traditions that all illness, to some extent, comes from being out of balance with the universe, from not knowing our place in the world. I think this is especially true of trauma. Trauma turns our world upside down and leads to unnerving changes in how we see ourselves in the world. It undermines our sense of safety—if we were lucky to have felt safe to begin with. Rather than the world being a frequently benevolent place, it becomes threatening and overwhelming and we can feel lost and broken. In order to heal from these kinds of wounds, we need to re-establish our place in the universe and find the kind of cosmic alignment that reminds us we belong, are loved, are safe and that we deserve good things. We do not talk about this kind of medicine often, but it is at the heart of so much of our pain.

Everything we need is inside of us. This takes some trust. And when we are at our most vulnerable, we are definitely not very trusting. It takes a little bit of experimentation and willingness to give up some pretty strong ideas about what we know about our own healing and wellness.

Star-gazing, like parsnips, goes in and out of fashion. All the same, I think it's one of my favourite ways to find that sense of quiet and calm we all have inside of us. Maybe next time you watch the stars, you can try and do some cosmic reconnecting. Maybe you will remember we have the ability to heal from many of our hurts (but not all of our hurts—please see above re: medical marvels and hospitals for hurts we need help with). And, depending on the night, you just might hear one of those eternal truths we often forget when we are hurt and cannot be reminded of too often when were well and whole: You are loved.

Squamish Matriarchy

Michelle Lorna Nahanee

*Michelle Lorna Nahanee kwi en sna, Eslhá7an uxwumixw, Sḵwx̱wú7mesh-
ulth uxwumixw.* My name is Michelle Lorna Nahanee, I was born in the
village of Eslhá7an, and I am a member of the Squamish Nation.

I celebrate my ability to introduce myself in my Ancestral language and
to know my home community as Eslhá7an, its Squamish place name. When
I was born in 1969, it was called Mission Reserve, and legally, it is still called
Mission Indian Reserve No. 1. Also, legally, I still have a Status Indian number
and card.

In 2018, I defended my thesis, "Decolonizing Identity – Indian Girl to
Squamish Matriarch," at Simon Fraser University. My work traces a trajectory of naming Indigeneity through my autoethnography. I have witnessed
immense changes in the power structures and political economy that have
governed both my grandmother's and my daughter's possibilities.

It has been a potent process for me to have the time and support to
deconstruct my own encumbrances. As a professional communicator, I
hope to make decolonizing practices more accessible to folks outside of
the academy. As a Matriarch, I have articulated critique because neocolonial
impacts are covert and systemic. They will need the love, care, commitment,
and reprimand of matriarchy to evolve beyond their current states.

My grandmother Eva May Nahanee and other Squamish women of her
era lived in second- and third-generation colonized lands now named North

Vancouver. They lost many family members to smallpox, lived with the violent criminalization of their spirituality, were confined within a highly regulated reserve system, and, of course, survived residential schools and the loss of their children—this is a shortened list of the atrocities they suffered.

But these women somehow held on to our songs, language, ceremonies, and teachings for us. They had the strength to operate in the harsh contact zone while still supporting their families—emotionally, spiritually, physically, and financially.

There is a great story in Squamish Elder Khot-La-Cha's book about his mother, Mary Capilano, paddling across an inlet to sell clams, berries, and baskets to the Hotel Vancouver. My grandmother Eva also wove cedar-root baskets and sold them with her delicious pies. Emily Carr writes about visiting Sophie Frank on Mission Reserve to buy her baskets and weavings. We have been doing business on this coast for centuries, though not in the self-centred capitalist sense. But Squamish women doing business is not the amazing part of the story. The best part of the story is the agency and power it took to stay Squamish under the overt, normalized violence of colonization. The strength of Squamish Matriarchs, past and present, continues to lift us.

L'hen Awtxw - Weaving Knowledge into the Future

Chief Janice George / Chepximiya Siyam

Chepximiya Siyam is my Ancestral name. My English name is Janice George. I am a Hereditary Chief from the George family of the Squamish Nation. I am a weaver. Weaving has always been so important to our people. Our women supported families with weavings—by weaving baskets, robes, and blankets. The women supported our people with commerce. There are stories of our women paddling across the water with their baskets full of clams and selling them in Vancouver to the Vancouver Hotel, which would also buy their baskets. The women supported their own families and other families. So those times are a little bit hard for us to imagine now.

We think about our Ancestors and our People whom we are descendants of. I like the way my husband puts it—*those people that came through the keyhole where there were thousands of us.* And then in my lifetime alone, we went down to two hundred people. Now we are back up to over four thousand people. When you think about how tenuous things can be, in my family alone, we lost a whole family to smallpox. My great-great-grandfather had a brother, and they had nine children and a wife. The whole family passed away. So now, our family is no longer one of the larger families for our people.

When I was growing up, my parents and grandparents always taught my sisters and I about our culture and the Land we live on. We would go for rides to Squamish, and my father would point out the people we were related to and explain how we were related to them. We would go to the fishing river, and he would say, "This is Jacob's Landing. This is where your great-great-grandfather fished. And that's where that family goes to fish." So, all of those things are still here. They are still alive today. We have to remember that.

So I teach my grandson, when he goes to the river: "You have to take care of that river. That's your river—you take care of it; you keep it clean." And he repeats my words to his mother. So we are still carrying on those things when we are taking care of our Land. And we think about the Land and our Ancestors who walked on it. Their DNA is still on that. Because we are always taught that when you have a problem or you are worried about something or you don't know the answer, go to the cedar tree. Lean on the cedar tree, sit and lean back on the cedar tree, and that cedar tree will give you the answers. You will get the answer sitting with that cedar tree. So we know our Ancestors' DNA is still on the Land.

At one point, the Dalai Lama came to visit because he wanted to talk to our spiritual people. We were lucky enough to be invited to that. The Dalai Lama and his monks met with our spiritual people. And the Dalai Lama said he still felt those prayers on the Land—they are still there on the land for us. I really believe that and feel that. They encourage me to do the work that I do. That is a big encouragement for me. It means a lot to me to be able to do the work that I do. It is something that I feel like it is not only a responsibility, but it comes from my heart to teach people. People need to learn because they need to have that feeling as well. We must pass on those words that were passed on to us. Growing up, those were the things I heard.

In 1981, we lost our family—we lost four of our family. We lost our parents and a sister and my son. I talk about that because my grandmother stepped into her role: my grandmother was right there. She passed away when she was ninety-eight, and she was born in 1910. She was brought up by her mother and her grandmother, so she had connections to pre-contact times, including teachings from before contact when we were living on the Land and teaching each other. So, we are really fortunate to have that.

But when we look now and do demographics about our homes and reserves, sadly and unfortunately, a lot of people are passing away quite young. For me, at sixty, now, I'm almost one of the Elders. That is not very old—sometimes, I feel pretty immature. But we need those teachings, and we must share them to continue to be who we are. We are the stewards of this Land. We can and we do contribute to society in a way that I feel like we are just starting now. People are talking about the medicines people make, the salves people make, the teas people make, and the weavings we are making now. The carvings, we have always seen them.

We are looking back now, and we are pulling things forward. But it is in a new way. For example, in my museum work, I travelled around the world with my husband to study our weavings. We would also see carvings that mostly men did. And they would say, well, that one was done by the great carver Floyd Joseph. This one was done by the Haida carver Bill Reid. And so, people would show us, 'wow, this is who made this', 'this is who made that'. And then they would lay out the weavings for us to look at. They were just so magnificent and so beautiful and so full of prayers and good energy and so full of love. But there are no names for them, so we don't know who their magnificent artists are. So, it is a different time for women now. We are helping to lead the way, and we are more open with our teachings. As Coast Salish People, as women, but also as Coast Salish People, we are sharing more with the world. We have something good to share. We have some help for people.

I talk about losing my family and my grandmother stepping in because she gave us a foundation to stand on. She shared the Culture. For every single event that happens in your life, if there is a traumatic event, there is a way to take care of yourself with the Culture and the Traditions we have—there is somewhere to go; there is a foundation to stand on. And I think one of the most important things about our Culture and our Traditions is that it takes care of us. It is like when we have food burnings for our Elders, and we offer them food. Our Ancestors who have left this world, if we still know how to take care of them, they can still take care of us. But we must reach out and do that work.

As Coast Salish People, we have a lot to share: Because I have been through hard times, I have used the Culture as a foundation to stand on. We teach the Culture to our children because they need that foundation as well. And sharing it with the world can help the world, so we have a lot to offer.

I always wanted to be a weaver—always, always, always wanted to be a weaver. Ever since I first saw that picture of the Chiefs wearing their robes when they were going to England to see the King and talk about our Land issues. They were worried about us then. I always wanted to weave. I didn't find somebody to teach me until later in life. We travelled to Skokomish, Washington, to learn. We learned from Bruce Miller, Subiyay—he is gone now—and Susan Pavel. We were really fortunate that he was still here. He was an Elder and a master weaver. As soon as we learned to make something, we rushed home, ran over to our grandmothers, and said, "Look—look what we know how to do." She went, "Ah, yes, yes, yes." And so, she started talking about the weavings and what the weavings are for. The weavings are protection, but not just against the cold. The weavings are for spiritual protection, protection against any kind of bad energy that might be sent to you. That is why weavers are weavers—that is what weavers do; that is the weavers' job in the community.

When we started teaching, we were able to access the information my grandmother carried and passed on for us. So now we know what the weavers do in the community, and we are telling weavers when we teach them—*You are weaving this for protection for whoever is going to wear this. Who are you weaving it for?* Speaking of weavings in our Ceremonies, weavings are the first thing that happens in a Ceremony when you are getting a name, or a Chieftainship, or getting married, or memorializing someone, or receiving Puberty Rights. And now, we have a new Ceremony for welcoming babies. The first thing they do is bring you out to the floor and there's all these people, and they put you on a blanket. A weaver made that blanket for you to stand on, a pure blanket. It represents purity because you are starting a new life in this new way—with this new name, this new title, this new partner, this new baby. That is how important the blanket is. Then they cover you with a robe and put a headband on you, and that has a job as well—to keep you focused on the work you are doing. When you do a beautiful good work, you are honouring your family, and you are honouring your Ancestors. This is not just for you.

So, we think about the Ancestors when we do this work because we are carrying their names. How important is that? I was able to—in my travels, while we were teaching, and all this other stuff was going on—go to Gatineau to the National Museum. I found out that we had Ancestors there. We had two Ancestors there. I phoned home and talked to our politicians, and they said to start the work—start doing the repatriation; we must bring them home. So, we started doing that work. I love this story because I think it should be a movie! What happened? We had to write out letters, sixty-seven actually, to sixty-seven different Nations and Tribes, to say, *Hey, we have these Ancestors, and they are at the museum in Gatineau. We are going to bring them home. Are you okay with that?* Then we had to wait six months. If anybody, any Tribe or Nation wrote back and said no, nope, those are ours, then it would have stopped everything. So we waited for six months, and nobody said anything. Nobody wrote a letter back or anything. So we gathered up some of our Spiritual Leaders in our community—our Medicine Man, a youth, and Chiefs—and went to get our Ancestors. We went to get them and what happened was, it was later in the evening when we had finished the Ceremony to wrap them. Our weavers had weaved blankets to wrap them in for bringing them home. Our carvers had made beautiful bent boxes for them to be brought home in as well. The museum was about to close, and they said, "Well, you're going to have to take them with you now because your plane in the morning leaves before we open." So, I took those Ancestors with me to the hotel room, and they slept in their bed. I kind of slept with one eye open—*Got anything to say?* But it went well, and it was beautiful.

When we got home, we had a police escort, and people met us at the airport. We put our Ancestors in the car and took them through Stanley Park. That is where they came from—they were taken from Stanley Park. And those Ancestors were at least four thousand years old. They were a man and a woman, and they had their foreheads wrapped, so their foreheads were slanted, which means they were high people. They were high Squamish people. So, we took them through the park, and the weather was just beautiful—it was sunshiny and warm. I think it was October. We got them home, but of course, before we did all that, we asked the Spirits, "Well, what should we do? What should we do for these Ancestors? How are we going to take care of our Ancestors?" And they said, *We're going to do everything for them. Everything we have, we're going to do it for them. We're going to do Catholic; we're going to do Shaker; we're going to do mask; we're going to do everything for those ancestors.* So we did, and it was a beautiful day.

My grandmother was still here then. I sat with my grandmother, and she said, "I want you to take me up and see them." So, we had prayers for them, and I went and walked up there with her. She was holding my arm, and she was little, tiny. We stood there and looked at them, and I felt smaller than a speck of sand looking at these at least four-thousand-year-old Ancestors. I thought, you loved me—you loved me back then. It is so amazing when you think about it. Their prayers are still here, and they loved us. They thought about us. They took care of the land for us.

I don't understand how we do not do the job we were taught to do. How do we not do that? Our weavers were able to weave the wrap for our Ancestors, and we brought them to be reburied, and we had Ceremony for them. It was a beautiful day. Then we went up to where we were burying them, and we had a snowstorm. We had a huge snowstorm, and a lot of people could not even make it through the road because of the snow. And while we were burying them, the eagles and the ravens were flying around together. It was so quiet, so beautiful. You could feel them there—it was amazing to have weaving a part of that—it is a part of it; you cannot separate it all. You cannot even separate it from the rest of what we do. And to think that it was almost gone once.

In 2003, when we started teaching, we had only one weaver. I am so proud that together we have taught over 2,400 people. And we are able to teach them what it means to be a weaver. I think that is such a privilege. And it is really a privilege to share with you what it means to do what we do. I just wanted to share all of this with you. What do I think is to come? I think we are going to share some more. We are going to keep on sharing. If we teach in the schools, we are teaching somebody who might be mayor when they grow up, and they will appreciate the First Nations and Indigenous People and what they do. And it might bring healing to other people, and that's important—to help each other, show love for each other. And that was what the Dalai Lama said, "Those prayers are still here. Those Ancestors' prayers are still here. I can feel those prayers." And they are, and I think it is our responsibility to do the same—to be like them. That is what we hear the Elders say. They are talking to you, so be like them. If you take an Ancestral name, you be like that Ancestor. Learn what that Ancestor did, and you do it, too. That is what it means to have a name. That is what it means to weave. And that is what it means to me to pass on the information and share.

Adapted from my EMMA Talk in Vancouver, BC, Oct 19, 2017:
http://emmatalks.org/video/chief-janice-george-chepximiya-siyam/

My Journey to Islamic Feminism

By dr. amina wadud

I begin as I always begin—in the name of Allah, whose grace I seek in this and all other matters. Throughout my life and in my work, I have often had to choose between three dominant inclinations in my own being: The first is my spirituality—I am a Sufi. Second is my academic or intellectual part: I am really into abstract ideas, especially theology, as seen in the books I write. Third, I am an activist. This last part has become the most important to me. I will tell you about key moments in my life and how they intersect with discourses about Islamic feminism. Obviously, I am a Muslim woman.

I was born in Maryland. My father was a Methodist minister who raised me in a God-conscious household. I had a kind of fascination and love for my father because he was a man who was able to stay consistent in what he said and believed. A lot of people experience some kind of betrayal in their faith of birth, but I did not have that experience.

I used to be afraid of thunderstorms. I believed God was having a conversation with me about all the little quirks in my life, things I hadn't quite got right. The thunder seemed to answer my questions. Once, during a thunderstorm, my father sat me in his lap and told me the biblical story about the rainbow—God's promise never again to destroy the world by water. It was my first experience of transcendence, the possibility of both fear and love coming together at a single point.

I was raised with the God of love. Consequently, when I became Muslim,

I took the name Wadud, which is an attribute of Allah that means loving. Even as a teenager, I knew not everyone worshipped in the same way. I became very curious about how people worship in other faiths. Away from my family during high school, I lived with people who were Jewish, Unitarian Universalist, and Catholic. By the time I entered the University of Pennsylvania as an undergraduate, I had become interested in religious practices from Eastern religious traditions. Eventually, I became a Buddhist. I lived in a Buddhist ashram and learned meditation, which I still practice. From meditation, I take away the idea that sometimes we must stop and breathe in the reality of the sacred—or take the spirit into everything that we do, if that spirit is to sustain us through all life's trials. However, all these doors seemed to lead me in a certain direction.

When I stepped into Islam, on Thanksgiving Day 1972, it was an auspicious entry. I immersed myself by reading every book about Islam I could find in the undergraduate library. Five months later, I was given a copy of the Qur'an, and I fell in love. This was only an English translation, though. I became motivated to remove the obstacles between myself and the text, so for more than ten years, I studied Arabic. I lived twice in Arabic-speaking parts of the world. My second time living abroad was in Egypt for an intensive advanced immersive study of languages and as progress toward my master's and Ph.D. in Qur'anic studies:

I remember a pivotal moment with a one-on-one tutor from the University of Cairo. He used to sit with me so we could read the Qur'an together—he would explain meaning. One time, we came across a passage about female slaves—concubines. When he gave me his interpretation, nothing in my gut accepted what he was saying, and nothing in my head understood how he drew that understanding from the original text. When I questioned him, our interaction became an issue of power and control. He acted as if I had questioned his competence and qualifications. He literally said, 'I'm a scholar. I've studied this many years, and I know this much.' For me, this was pivotal—I began to understand interpretation must follow a method: one must be clear about methodology in order to confirm the goals you they seek or in order to attest to the truth of their interpretation.

I also came to understand that as a woman my experiences might lead to something another reader, even a scholar, would not experience. This understanding compelled me to pursue my Ph.D, in reading for gender in the Qur'an. The results of my Ph.D dissertation became my first book, *Qur'an and Woman*.

Qur'an and Woman came out in 1992, while I was an assistant professor at the International Islamic University in Malaysia. I was unaware at the time that the book would become a primary text of Islamic feminism. At that time, I was not even a feminist. I found serious problems in the dominant discourse of feminism, especially given my identities as an African American woman, as a woman who was not only a Muslim, but who sought to visibly affirm that identity by wearing the hijab in public. I was also trying to make my way in a field of study with only male teachers.

In my heart, I felt something through the text; I experienced something, but there wasn't a bridge to help me negotiate between the patriarchal expectations and the often very white, academic context of Islamic studies. I insisted that because the Qur'an promises itself for all times, and all places, and all people, then it is also making a promise to me. Sometimes I did not find myself in the legacy of fourteen hundred years of Qur'anic study. Indeed, until the 20th century there was no written record of women's experiences with or interpretations of the Qur'an. No exegesis (interpretation of the holy text). We know women read it, and we know they memorized it, but where was the legacy of their discourse about it? Where was the engagement with it from a female perspective? This is one reason my little book, *Qur'an and Woman*, has been translated into a dozen languages. This is why it is still relevant today: it is an experience of the Qur'an through the methodologies of Qur'anic study from a woman's perspective.

After I completed my Ph.D., my first job was assistant professor in the International Islamic University in Malaysia. When I went to Malaysia, Allah opened an amazing door for me. Within one month, I began meeting with a group of eight women who would form the non-government organization Sisters in Islam. We were wedded to the idea that what we were experiencing on a day-to-day basis, as Muslim women, was not necessarily because of our religion. We decided that we needed to spend more time looking at the places where there was a rupture to understand where this rupture had come in. We also became active producing new knowledge and changing the way the conversation was going. This became especially important when we, collectively, went to the 1995 Beijing Global Conference for Women. That conference pivotally expressed what would continue for the next ten or twenty years. There were more Muslim women present at that forum than at any such forum before or after. The dominant voices there highlighted differences among Muslim women—differences that would shape the discourse about Islam and women for a very long time.

With the success of the Iranian Revolution in 1979, what we now know as *political Islam* or *Islamists* began to see itself as a viable possibility. The women associated with Islamism and interested in creating an Islamic state told others about the wisdom of Islam's position on women. In other words, for them, Islam was already fixed: it was perfect and patriarchal. They were adamant that you cannot have Islam and human rights, or Islam and feminism. They were in total agreement with the other dominant voice at Beijing, which I now call *secular Muslim feminism*. Because, there are Muslims who are secular, and there are feminists who are secular and Muslim. The secular Muslim feminists were adamant religion should not be part of the conversation on human rights, insisting that you cannot have both Islam and human rights. So, the Islamists said "our purview is going to be this fixed, patriarchal Islam," and the secular Muslim feminists said "our purview is going to be human rights." What's interesting is that there was a point of agreement between them. Yet, most Muslim women actually fall somewhere in between.

We, the Sisters of Islam, were really clear that we were also in between, but we did not have a methodology, a strategy, or even a set of objectives. We simply felt our position intuitively. So, what we had to do over the next ten or fifteen years was to make our location coherent. The secret was in the place where the two larger groups agreed: you cannot have both Islam and human rights, or Islam and feminism. This is because someone had already decided what both of those things meant. When we took agency to redefine feminism, keeping in mind global feminism had already entered into its third wave and was testifying to the significance of people's particular localities. They had joined a trend away from universalizing what all women experience. Instead, global feminism had begun considering that women experience particular things with regard to a number of different localities, all of which are significant, particularly when subjected to systemic patriarchal oppressions. So we moved into that aspect of feminism, a feminism that still breathes, and a feminism that can be challenged from within and from without. But the real litmus test came when we understood that whoever defines Islam, or whoever has the power to implement their definition of Islam, also had control over the conversation.

When we took agency to construct these definitions on our own, that was the beginning of what is now called *Islamic feminism*. It is a serious interrogation and participation in our own agencies with regard to our identities as both Muslim, and feminists. While that did not happen in 1995, it shows how Beijing was a starting point. You can see where the momentum was going.

By the time I had finished my book in 1992, I was too radical for the International Islamic University, so they did not renew my contract. But having met the women who became Sisters in Islam, I had gained a different sense of the significance of my contribution. Although I still loved abstract reasoning and theology, Sisters in Islam connected me to a movement that would be taken up in earnest by the twenty-first century.

Muslim women have reached a critical mass. In no place and in no time do women themselves *not* take some agency to control how they are being represented; how the religions is being defined, and how they assert their own agency. If that means they must tackle Islam's patriarchal definitions, they are prepared to do so—through scholarship, spirituality, art, and activism. If it means they must take on feminism, Islamophobia, and certain forms of aggressive secularism, then they take that on, too. This combination is going on everywhere—in every little town, in every village, and every country you can think of, women are on the move. We are a force to be reckoned with. We will not be pushed back. So it is amazing to be living now and to be a part of it all—to feel that collective push.

I am also humbled by the experience of being a part of this setting in which Muslim women from diverse circumstances had an opportunity to meet, but I could not get over what made us different from each other well enough to actually begin to come together. So, from the days since the Beijing conference, I have developed even greater respect for difference. Working through our differences is one of the most important challenges Muslim women face, especially given the nature of some conservative governments that are now at the helm. They want us divided. They want Black people to go against white people. They want Muslims to go against Jews. They want women to go against men. They want queers to go against straights. They want a divide. When we come to embrace diversity as part of the beauty of what it means to be human, and in my case what it means to be Muslim, it'll be easier for us to stand together to challenge the forces that actually have the most to gain by our divide. is what I learned from participating in the Muslim women's movement.

In 1994, when Nelson Mandela was in office for one hundred days, I was invited to Cape Town, South Africa. There, I did a lecture tour, presented at a conference about Islamic reform, and visited the townships and different parts of the country. They loved that I was Black, a woman, and a scholar. The discussion came to have me step into the role of the *khatib*, the person who gives the Friday sermon. August 1994 was the beginning of a serious change for me. I never imagined that I would give a Friday sermon or lead mixed-gender prayers before this discussion.

I know Allah is present everywhere, so any time I pray, no matter where I stand, I am praying directly to Allah. So, it doesn't matter if I am praying in the closet, the grass, my house, or at the mosque, because I am always praying directly to Allah. But, when they proposed the possibility of my giving a *Khutbah*, I realized that in my security of personal worship I was not taking responsibility for what it means comprehensively. If Allah really is everywhere and can recognize any prayer anywhere in any form, then why would I not step forward and lead the prayer?

So, the Khutbah I gave in 1994 centers a woman's particular experiences as a marker for Islam for the whole community. I have sometimes attended

Friday prayers where the Khutbah is all about guy stuff, with absolutely nothing to do about me. Still I am supposed to listen and be moved. I am not really feeling it, so what's going on? Yes, guys experiences are a part of the human experience. But sometimes it is not really a part of my experience as a woman. And that is okay. As long as there is an opportunity for other humans, who are women to speak from their experiences and for everyone else to listen. That's what I learned since 1994. Thing is, there was a still small voice inside that said, "Not you. It is not supposed to be you," so for the next eleven years, I researched and did soul searching: "Can it be me?" People would ask me to lead prayer in small settings, but I always said no. Because, inside, I was still saying, "No, it's not supposed to be me."

In 2005, I was ready. I will tell you something about what made me ready. Remember what I said about being in Beijing—how women there were unable to work out their differences to consolidate their efforts into a single goal? That it was much more important for them to defend their particular location? That really had me thinking about diversity is beautiful. How then to make it into a seamless whole? How do we see the harmony and the beauty in our complexity and difference? For me, harmony and beauty rests in Tawhid. Tawhid is the Arabic word used to express Islamic monotheism—Allah as one. But Tawhid comes from the emphatic second form of the verb: something that puts other things into motion, from multiplicity toward unity. So I came up with a Tawhidic paradigm, which I discuss more and more in my work, and I also write about it more.

As I said before, Allah is everywhere, and yet as a Muslim, we consider our acknowledgement of the reality of Allah to be one of the primary aspects of our belief. It is in our Shahadah, or profession of faith, La ilaha ill-Allah, I bear witness—there is no God but the God. Focusing on the oneness of God is a principal part of how we identify ourselves. Because Tawhid as an active term, meaning: the making of one from many. It is also a principal motivation for social justice—unconditional equality and reciprocity.

When I came up with the Tawhidic paradigm, I was working mostly on gender within the context of the heteronormative binary—which is where I still felt most afflicted in terms of my spiritual and intellectual development as an academic and activist. This dual role helped me understand how tawhid should be put into practice. This Tawhidic paradigm motivated me to think through theology into the reform movement and with the critical mass of Muslim women. I love talking about the Tawhidic paradigm because when Muslims come to the discussion table, they are already secure in the idea about tawhid as the oneness of Allah we all believe in. When Muslim women and other disenfranchised, marginalized members of our community are looking for a way to align that belief into the important social justice work they do, the Tawhidic paradigm brings it all together. Tawhid allows me to understand the good in your heart is better when you put it into action in your body—when you embody what you believe. So in 2005, when I was asked if I would lead the prayer, I was ready and said yes. And the rest is history.

Sometimes it is a history that I cannot go beyond. Some people think I am a kind of "wind-up imam" and want to lead prayer everywhere I go. What it really means to me from that time forward, and what it should mean to everyone, is if you know how to pray, even in the most rudimentary forms, you are already an imam. So when I look back to the place where I walked up to the *mimbar* in Cape Town, South Africa, I am clear: wherever I stand to perform my prayers, I stand directly in front of Allah.

Because we are political beings connected to networks of other political beings, it was necessary for me to stand forward and make an embodied affirm-ation of what I believe, even in situations that actually is a little uncomfortable. For this is not the kind of thing one should take lightly. There are consequences when you do something like stand for Muslim ritual leaders. But I was ready.

When the prayer service was so widely publicized in 2005, I was still not a feminist. I still said I was "pro-faith" and "pro-feminism." But then something happened with the Tawhidic paradigm that shifted how I engaged Islamic theology. One of the most important was the launching of the Musawah Movement in 2009.

Musawah is an Arabic word that means equality and reciprocity. It principally addresses the mechanisms that maintain structures of Muslim women's subordination, such as the forms of Muslim Personal Status Law or Muslim family law in many nation states. One of the residuals from colonialism is the implementation of Muslim Personal Status Law giving a legal structure to certain aspects of Islamic laws within that nation-state. Muslim Personal Status Laws perpetuate social imbalances, in terms of gender and family. So, while this was a compensation given by the colonizers as an indication of compliance with Muslim sentiment, since then, by allowing certain aspects of Islam to remain in practice, what really happens is that Muslim Personal Status Law (MPL) has become the legal structures that violate women's possibilities of making changes in their lives. In other words, MPL is set up on the basis of a gender hegemony. Our question is, what part of this law is Islamic? After all is said and done, MPL is a construct used to maintain male privilege. For while the classical legal developments of Islamic law were complex they did not question the subaltern status of women, and patriarchy was encoded in how they constructed law and legal theory. We now know this. We also know men's ways of being and knowing—patriarchy and male privilege—did not start with Islam and will not end with Islam. We must root it out comprehensively throughout the entire world.

After my prayer in 2005, I published my second book, *Inside the Gender Jihad, Women's Reform in Islam*. For me, that title's key word is *inside*. I focus on the interior part of gender reform because I think of it as a complete trajectory. In a *hadith qudsi*, Allah calls us to know ourselves—to know yourself deeply is the means for you to know your Lord. When you know your Lord, you want to live in such a way that everything is in accordance with the order and beauty of the entire universe. That is the gift you give when your heart is open to that level of love.

I understand one reason why it is difficult for some Muslims to claim the word *feminism* is its historical links to imperialism. However, when Muslim women step up and demand recognition, equality, and justice, we have already changed the script from other times in history when justice was a kind of benevolence on the part of those with privilege. Now, we understand justice as equality for all of humankind. When Musawah was launched, I came out as a feminist. The only way for the unconditional call for justice in Islam to be fulfilled is for Muslim women to experience that justice. This means, the lived realities of Muslim women and other marginalized Muslims becomes the measurement for the fulfillment of Islam.

Why is it that the definition of Islam for so many people is frozen somewhere back in time, or some other place? Why is Islam not here and now? Are we all not also makers of Islam? The launching of Musawah reminded me to take ownership with regard to every aspect of my experiences as a Muslim, a woman, and an African American. And in every context.

We think rituals only happen in the mosque and with men. And there is a lot that happens there as well. But we have to come to a place where we also understand that everything is viewed with spirit. What kind of agent are you on the earth when your actions are informed by the spirit of what you bring to it? For me, this is the essence of both Islam and feminism. So, it is not possible to be a Muslim except as a feminist. It is not possible for me to be a feminist except as a Muslim, and each of us have a possibility of participating in it.

This essay is an adaption of my EMMA Talk in Vancouver, BC in May 2018. http://emmatalks.org/video/dr-amina-wadud/

Two Stories

Leanne Betasamosake Simpson

I want to share four inter-related stories from within the wisdom and intelligence of my homeland, because I work as a spoken-word artist, a writer, an academic and an activist, and I want to use all of those vehicles to say something about decolonizing gender. [In the original EMMA Talk Leanne presented four stories. Two of them are included here.]

STORY #1

Story #1 is a very, very old traditional Mississauga Nishnaabeg story that on one hand is about the origin of maple syrup/sugar, and on the other hand, it's about something else altogether. Today my version of this story is called *Binoojiinh Makes a Lovely Discovery*. *Binoojiinh* means *child*, and Binoojiinh's preferred gender pronouns in English are they/their. One of the responsibilities storytellers carry is to make sure the stories are relevant to people, that people can see themselves in the story, that stories are a "coming in" to Nishinaabeg intelligence and nationhood, and this means telling our stories from all angles, from all different perspectives. Stories in Nishnaabeg thought are spirits that shift in order to illuminate what we don't know. They are coded messages and our responsibility both individually and collective is to decipher the layered meanings of story as we move through our own lives. A lot of times, our stories get positioned

as one dimensional legends or myths told as simplistic narratives devoid of
conceptual thought and Anishinaabeg genius because this fits into the colonial narrative that Indians are dumb and that our knowledge systems are
quaint and from another time, and that we are not theoretical or complex
and that if we want to prove that we are intelligent, we have to be able to
master Western theory and intellectual traditions.
I'm not falling for that.

Binoojiinh is out walking in the bush one day
It is Ziigwan
the lake is opening up
the goon was finally melting
they are feeling that first warmth of spring on their cheeks
"Nigitchi nendam," they are thinking, "I'm happy."

Then that Binoojiinh who is out walking
collecting firewood for their Doodoom
decides to sit under Ninaatigoog
maybe just stretch out
maybe just have a little rest
maybe gather firewood a little later
"Owah, Ngitchi nendam nongom.
I'm feeling happy today," says that Binoojiinh.

And while that Binoojiinh
is lying down, and looking up
they see Ajidamoo up in the tree
"Bozhoo Ajidamoo! I hope you had a good winter."
"I hope you had enough food cached."
But Ajidamoo doesn't look up because she's already busy.
She's not collecting nuts.
Gawiin.
She's not building their nest
Gawiin, not yet.

She's not looking after any young.
Gawiin, too early.
She's just nibbling on the bark, and then doing some sucking.

Nibble, nibble suck.
Nibble, nibble suck.
Nibble, nibble, suck.
Nibble, nibble, suck.

Binoojiinh is feeling a little curious.
So they do it too, on one of the low branches.

Nibble, nibble suck.
Nibble, nibble suck.
Nibble, nibble, suck.
Nibble, nibble, suck.

MMMMMMMMmmmmmm.
This stuff tastes good.
It's real, sweet water.
MMMMMmmmmmmmmmm.

Then Binoojiinh gets thinking
and they make a hole in that tree
and they make a little slide for
that sweet water to run down
they make a quick little container
out of birch bark, and
they collect that sweet water
and they take that sweet water home
to show their mama.

That doodoom is excited and she has three hundred questions:

"Ah Binoojiinh, what is this?"
"Where did you find it?"

"Which tree"
"Who taught you how to make it?"
"Did you put semaa?"
"Did you say miigwech?"
"How fast is it dripping?"
"Does it happen all day?"
"Does it happen all night?"
"Where's the firewood?"

Binoojiinh tells their doodoom the story.
She believes every word
because they are her Binoojiinh
and they love each other very much.
"Let's cook the meat in it tonight,
it will be lovely sweet"
"Nahow."
"Nahow."

So they cooked that meat in that sweet water
it was lovely sweet
it was extra lovely sweet
it was even sweeter than just that sweet water.

The next day, Binoojiinh takes their mama
to that tree and their mama brings Nokomis
and Nokomis brings all the Aunties, and
there is a very big crowd of Michi Saagiig Nishnaabekwewag
and there is a very big lot of pressure
Binoojiinh tells about Ajidamoo
Binoojiinh does the nibble nibble suck part.

At first there are technical difficulties
and none of it works,
but Mama rubs Binoojiinh's back
she tells Binoojiinh that she believes them anyway

they talk about lots of variables like heat and temperature and time
then Giizis comes out and warms everything up
and soon its drip
                    drip
                        drip
                            drip

those Aunties go crazy
Saasaakwe!
dancing around
hugging a bit too tight
high kicking
and high fiving
until they take it back home
boil it up
boil it down
into sweet, sweet sugar.

Ever since, every Ziigwan
those Michi Saagiig Nishnaabekwewag
collect that sweet water
and boil it up
and boil it down
into that sweet, sweet sugar
all thanks to Binoojiinh and their lovely discovery,
and to Ajidamoo and her precious teaching
        and to Ninaatigoog and their boundless sharing.

....

This spring, while tapping a stand of maple trees, I remembered that this
is one of my favorite stories. It's one of my favorites because nothing
violent happens in it. At every turn, Binoojiinh is met with very basic, core
Nishnaabeg values: love, compassion and understanding. They centre their

day around their own freedom and joy—I imagine myself at seven running through a stand of maples with the first warmth of spring marking my cheeks with warmth. I imagine everything good in the world. My heart, my mind and my spirit are open and engaged and I feel as if I could accomplish anything. I imagine myself grasping at feelings I haven't felt before: that maybe life is so good that it is too short; that there really isn't enough time to love everything.

In reality, I have to image myself in this situation, because as a child, I don't think I was ever in a similar situation. My experience of education from kindergarten to graduate school was one of coping with someone else's agenda, curriculum, and pedagogy, someone who was neither interested in my well-being as a Binoojiinh, my connection to my homeland, my language or history, or my Nishnaabeg intelligence. No one ever asked me what I was interested in nor did they ask for my consent to participate in their system. My experience of education was one of continually being measured against a set of principles that required surrender to an assimilative colonial agenda in order to fulfill those principles. I distinctly remember being in Grade 3 at a class trip to the sugar bush and the teacher showing us two methods of making maple syrup—the pioneer method which involved a black pot over an open fire and clean sap, and the "Indian method," which involved a hollowed-out log in an unlit fire, with large rocks in the log to heat the sap up—sap which had bark, insects, dirt and scum over it. The teacher asked us which method we would use; being the only native kid in the class, I was the only one that chose the "Indian method".

Things are different for this Binoojiinh. They have already spent seven years immersed in a nest of Nishnaabeg intelligence that normalizes a spectrum of genders and sexual orientations in a web of diversity.

They already understand the importance of observation and learning from our animal teachers when they watch the squirrel so carefully, and then mimic her actions. They understands embodiment and conceptual thought when they then takes this observation and applies it to their own situation—by making a cut in the maple tree and using a cedar shunt. They rely upon their own creativity to invent new technology. They patiently wait for the sap to collect. They take that sap home and shares it with their family. Their mother in turn, meets Binoojiinh discovery with love and trust. Binoojiinh watches as their mama used the sap to boil the deer meat for supper. When they taste the deer, the sweetness, they learn about reduction, and when they go to clean the pot, they learn about how sap can be boiled into sugar. Binoojiinh then takes the Elders to the tree already trusting that they will be believed, that their knowledge and discovery will be cherished and that they will be heard.

Binoojiinh learned a tremendous amount over a two-day period—self-led, driven by both their own curiosity and their own personal desire to learn. They learn to trust themselves, their family and their community. They learned the sheer joy of discovery. They learned how to interact with the spirit of the maple. They learned both from the land and with the land. They learned what it felt like to be recognized, seen and appreciated by their community. They come to know maple sugar with the support of family and Elders. They came to know maple sugar in the context of love.

To me, this is what coming into wisdom within an Michi Saagiig Nishnaabe context looks like—it takes place in the context of family, community and relation. It lacks overt coercion and authority, values so normalized within mainstream western pedagogy that they are rarely ever critiqued. The land, aki, is both context and process. The process of coming to know is learner-led and profoundly spiritual in nature. Coming to know is the pursuit of whole body intelligence practiced in the context of freedom and when realized collectively it generates generations of loving, creative, innovative, self-determining, inter-dependent and self-regulating community minded individuals. It creates communities of individuals with the capacity to uphold and move forward our political traditions and systems of governance

It is critical to avoid the assumption that this story takes place in pre-colonial times because Nishnaabeg conceptualizations of time and space present an ongoing intervention to linear thinking—this story happens in various incarnations all over our territory every year in March when the Nishnaabeg return to the sugar bush.

Binoonjiinh's very presence shatters the erasure of Indigenous peoples from settler consciousness.

Binoonjiinh also escapes the rigidity of colonial gender binaries by having influence and agency within their family, while physically disrupting settler colonial commodification and ownership of the land through the implicit assumption that they are supposed to be there.

Their existence as a hub of intelligent Nishnaabeg relationality may be threatened by land theft, environmental contamination, residential schools and state run education, and colonial gender violence, but Binoojiinh is there anyway, making maple sugar as they always have done, in a loving compassionate reality, propelling us to recreate the circumstances within which this story and Nishnaabewin takes place. Propelling us to rebel against the permanence of settler colonial reality and not just "dream alternative realities" but to create them, on the ground in the physical world in spite of being occupied. If we accept colonial permanence, then our rebellion can only take place withinside settler colonial thought and reality, and we also become too willing to sacrifice the context that creates and produces people like Binoojiinh.

What if Binoojiinh had no access to the sugar bush because of land dispossession, environmental contamination or global climate change?

What if the trauma and pain of ongoing colonial gendered violence had made it impossible for their mama to believe them or for their mama to reach out and so gentle rub their lower back at that critical point? What if that same trauma and pain prevented their aunties and elders to gather around them and supported them when there were technical difficulties? What if settler–colonial parenting strategies positioned the child as "less believable" than an adult?

What if Binoojiinh had been in a desk at a school that didn't honour at its core their potential within Michi Saagiig Nishnaabeg intelligence? Or if they had been in an educational context where having an open heart as a liability instead of a gift? What if they had not running around, exploring, experimenting, observing the squirrel . . . completely engaged in a Michi Saagiig Nishnaabeg ways of knowing? What if they hadn't been on the land at all?

What if Binoojiinh lived in a world where no one listens to girls or Two Spirit children or children? What if Binoojiinh because of the intense racism and discrimination targeting LGBT youth had succumbed to those pressures? What if Binoojiinh had been missing or murdered before they ever made it out to the sugar bush?

STORY #2

The brochure for Akiden Boreal is cluttered, the kind that has too much information in a font requiring dedicated commitment to read. But we all read it anyway, and saved it, and passed it around to our friends that get it, acting nonchalant for those that don't. We hovered over it while it passed from sweaty hand to sweaty hand, babysitting it until we can get it safely taped back onto the fridge, behind the magneted pile of shit we can't lose and have nowhere else to put.

Akiden means vagina, literally; I think it means "earth place" or "land place," but I'm not completely confident about the meaning of the "den" part of the word, and there is no one left to ask. I think about that word a lot because I approach my vagina as a decolonizing project and because metaphors are excellent hiding places.

The confirmation number for my reservation at Boreal Akiden is written on a slip of paper, scotch taped to the fridge, behind the brochure that is also taped to the fridge, hidden in plain sight. It is for three hours on June 21. I also memorized the confirmation number because I was confident I'd lose the slip, and so on the same day I scratched it into the right front bumper of my car in case of early onset dementia. I'm not good at looking after important pieces of paper, so I also wrote it on the eavestrough on the left side of the house because houses are harder to lose than paper, and no one will think to look there. The number is ten years old now, booked on the blind faith of youth, in hopes that I'd have enough of a credit rating to borrow the money to pay for the three hours. Blind faith rarely pays off, but this time it did, and I do. Barely. The bank says it will take me the rest of my life to pay off the loan, but it doesn't matter. No one gives a shit about owing money anymore.

I've read and reread the Boreal Akiden brochure every night for the past six months and so has Migizi. A combination of fear verging on horror mixes with fleeting placidity when I get to the "Tips For a Great Visit" section. I'm worried that I'll have a panic attack or some sort of a meltdown and fuck up my only chance in this place. The brochure warns in stilted legalese that there's a "sizable" percentage of people who visit the Akiden network and never recover. They spend the rest of their lives trying to get back in. This kind of desperation is a friend of mine and I know myself well enough to know that it is perhaps better not to play Russian roulette with myself like this and with Migizi. I also know myself well enough to know, I will.

When I asked Migizi to do this with me last year he said yes, seemingly without taking the time to feel the weight of "yes" on the decaying cartilage that barely holds life together. People do all kinds of shit in the Akiden network, and in the tiny moment he said yes, it was unclear what he was saying yes to, exactly. The network was initially set up for ceremony, but when people thought about it, there are all kinds of things we can't do anymore and all kinds of those things can be thought of as ceremony—having a fire, sharing food, making love, even just sitting with things for a few hours.

I decided ahead of time not to ask Migizi questions that I didn't want answers to, about our visit to the network, or about anything else. And you should know that I'm not sorry. We are from people that have been forced to give up everything and we have this one opportunity to give something to ourselves and we're going to take it. We are fucking taking it. Even though occupation anxiety has worn our self-worth down to frayed wires. Even though there is risk. After all, everything we are afraid of has already happened.

I arrived a day early in accordance to the anxiety management plan I made as was suggested in the brochure. I booked a massage at the hotel, spent some time in the sauna and steam room, ate leafy green vegetables, did yoga and cardio, just like a white lady. I'm still carrying a lot of frightened that the two of us will just be caught up in awkwardness and we won't be able to relax into this. The brochure suggested taking anxiety meds, and most people do because this is a more controlled strategy then self-medicating with drugs and alcohol. I want to be the kind of person that can melt into this and experience fully present. I want to be that kind of person, but I know at my core I'm not. I'm the kind of person that actually needs to self-medicate in order to not fuck up important things.

Migizi and I met at the hotel bar last night for a few drinks to reconnect before the visit. It was graceless at first for sure. But after the first bottle of wine I could see him breathing more easily. He stretched out his legs under the table and let them touch mine. My eye contact was less jolted. He seemed more confident as the night went on, and the silently voiced "you're not good enough" that marinates in the bones of my inner ear and pricks at my edges was a little quieter.

Now it's 10 AM and we've each had two cups of coffee, one at the hotel and one in the waiting room at the security check in for Akiden Boreal. You have to arrive two hours early before your scheduled appointment to make sure there is ample time for the scanning process. Last year some activists burnt down the tropical rainforest habitat by sneaking in an old style flint. They wanted open access, which I want too. But in the process, they disappeared the last members of the tropic rain forest choir.

I'm watching to see if Migizi is having the same reaction, but he is good at holding his cards close to his chest. He drank three shots of whisky from a silver flask outside the door before we came in. I had two because I'm desperate to be able to feel this place. I tell myself our Ancestors would be ok with that, because after all, we're going to be someone's Ancestors someday, and I'd want my grandchildren to do whatever they had to do to experience this. Compassion and empathy have to win at some point.

We clear security and wait in the holding room until the Watcher comes in to unlock the door to the site. She does so at exactly noon. I walk inside and am immediately hit with the smell of cedar. It's real cedar, not synthetic and according to the brochure that means it comes with a feeling, not just a smell. The brochure says to be prepared for feelings and to let them wash over you like the warm waves of the ocean. This is the key to a good visit the brochure insists.

I feel my body relaxing in spite of myself. The space seems immense even though I know my Ancestors would think this is ridiculous, us figuring out the smallest amount of habitat that could sustain itself and then putting in in big glass jar without a lid.

I feel like crying. Actually I'm starting to cry and I know Migizi hates that and I hate that too and so I'm biting my lip but silent tears are falling all over my face anyway. The brochure said that you can't take any expectations into the Akiden. That whatever happens, happens. That this could be your first and only time in the natural world and you just have to accept whatever experience you have. For some it's profoundly spiritual. For others it's just full on traumatic, and still others feel nothing. The brochure says that learning takes place either way. That the Akinomaaget will teach whatever way it goes.

Migizi licks the tears off my checks, takes my hand and we walk to the centre of Boreal Akiden, where there is a circle of woven cedar, like our Ancestors might have done on the floor of a lodge. He opens his hand and there are two tiny, red, dried berries in it. I ask. He says they are from his Kobade, his great grandmother and they are called "raspberries". He's says they are medicine and his family saved them for nearly 100 years in case one of them ever got into Boreal Akiden. I ask him if they are hallucinogens. He says he thinks so. I'm becoming overwhelmed in the same way the brochure warned us and so I decide to eat one. We both do. Within minutes, I'm more relaxed and happier than I've ever felt. I'm drowning in peacefulness and calm and there is a deep knife of sadness being forcefully pulled out of me.

Migizi reaches over and touches the skin on my lower back with just his fingertips. It feels like he's just moving the air very closest to my skin around. I'm losing track of my body, the edges are letting go and I'm a fugitive in a fragile vessel of feelings and smells and senses. My lungs draw in moist air to deeper reaches, my back is arching, my heart feels like it is floating out of my chest.

Then, Migizi lies down on the cedar bows, on his side, facing me. He puts his right hand on my cheek, and he kisses my lips. He's kissing my lips and in doing so he is touching that part of me I've never shared with anyone because I didn't know it was there. There is a yellow light around his body and I can feel it mixing with my light. Part of me is a pool of want. Part of me is a waterfall filling up that want almost faster than I can desire. At one point he stops and takes his clothes off, which he's never done before because he's afraid I will see his self-hatred, the self-hatred we both share and pretend doesn't exist. And we're there, in the middle of Boreal Akiden, in the middle of the moment the brochure warned us about. Naked. Embraced. Enmeshed. Crying. Completely convinced that being an Akiden addict for the rest of our lives is important, convinced that living as an addict, dying as an addict is unconditionally worth it. Convinced that breaking all of our healthy connections to the city, the concrete and even the movement, for the chance to be here one more time before we die, is worth it.

Because this is how our Ancestors would have wanted it.

....

The above essay is an excerpt from Leanne Simpson's EMMA Talk in Vancouver, BC, April 2015. http://emmatalks.org/video/leanne-simpson/

Story #1 was originally published as "Gwiizens Makes a Lovely Discovery" from The Gift Is in the Making: Anishinaabeg Stories *by Leanne Simpson, copyright © 2013 Leanne Simpson. Reprinted with permission of Portage & Main Press, Winnipeg.*

Story #2 was later published in her collection This Accident of Being Lost: Songs and Stories *by Leanne Betasamosake Simpson copyright © 2017 Leanne Betasamosake Simpson, used with permission of House of Anansi Press, Inc. Toronto. www.houseofanansi.com.*

Where do we get that belief that ordinary people can change the world? From the past. And from the present—from the kind and quality of stories around us. Not because I want heroes so much as I want intervention—but in a way I do want heroes, I want people to experience those emotions we don't talk about much, the emotions of public rather than private life, of hope, solidarity, joy, power, voice. Those emotions are themselves transformative; they bring you into a new sense of self or reward a self that's transformed itself by entering the public realm. – Rebecca Solnit

Acknowledgements

For their work on this book, my deepest gratitude goes to the entire team at TouchWood Editions—Taryn Boyd, Renée Layberry, Tori Elliott, and Colin Parks, as well as copy editor Sasha Braun and cover designer Tree Abraham. I also thank Tasnim Nathoo, Julie Flett, dr. amina wadud, Anoushka Ratnarajah, Astra Taylor, Berit Fischer, Christa Couture, Chief Janice George, Corin Browne, Dorothy Woodend, Helen Hughes, Jamie-Leigh Gonzales, Julie Martin, Kian Cham, Kinnie Starr, Leanne Betasamosake Simpson, Lara Messersmith-Glavin, Maneo Mohale, Margret Killjoy, Michelle Nahanee, Shaunga Tagore, Silvia Federici, Tasha Kaur, Vivek Shraya, Vivienne McMaster, Walidah Imarisha, Am Johal, Melissa Roach, the entire EMMA Talks team and all the EMMA speakers, the Cultural Unit, City of Vancouver, Arts in Action, Claudine Pommier, Tahia Ahmed, Melanie Matining, Rebecca Solnit, Terry Tempest Williams, bell hooks, Nick Montgomery, Sylvia McFadden, Jeanette Sheehy, Candice Wright, Hari Alluri, Chris Bergman, Liam Bergman, and Zach Bergman. And of course, Emma Goldman. Finally, thank you to all the readers and listeners, without whom there would be no point.

Notes

Image Credits

Page 6: EMMA Talks Logo designed by Joi Arcand

Page 7: Emma Goldman at Union Square in 1916 (public domain)

Page 43: Slave Mask: Image Reference, NW0191. Source: Jacques Arago, Souvenirs d'un aveugle. Voyage autour du monde par M. J. Arago. (Paris, 1839–40), vol. 1, facing p. 119.

Page 44: Ducking Stool, from a 17th century American Puritan pamphlet (image ID: M2BTHY). Alamy.

Page 94–103: Photos of Community Engaged Art by Vivienne McMaster

Pages 156, 159: "Inglorious Vegetables" and "Written in the Stars" illustrations by Tasnim Nathoo

List of Contributors

dr. amina wadud is professor emeritus of Islamic Studies and visiting scholar at Starr King School for the Ministry. She is the author of *Qur'an and Woman* and *Inside the Gender Jihad*. She is a founding member of Sisters in Islam and resource person for Musawah, the global movement for reform in Muslim Personal Status Law.

Anoushka Ratnarajah is a queer, mixed-race femme of Sri Lankan and British ancestry and an interdisciplinary and transnational artist and arts organizer. She has worked as a producer, performer, writer, facilitator and arts organizer with cultural and arts organizations in Vancouver, Montreal, and New York.

Astra Taylor is a documentary filmmaker, writer, activist, and musician. Her films include *Examined Life*, *Zizek!* and *What is Democracy?* Her recent books are *The People's Platform* and *Democracy May Not Exist, But We'll Miss It When It's Gone*. Astra was a fellow of the Shuttleworth Foundation for her work on challenging predatory practices around debt.

carla bergman is an independent scholar, filmmaker, and producer. She codirected the film *Common Notions: Handbook Not Required*, coedited the book *Stay Solid: A Radical Handbook For Youth*, and coauthored *Joyful Militancy: Building Thriving Resistance in Toxic Times*, both AK Press. carla spends much of her time with a camera, and walking with her partner, kids and friends in Vancouver, BC on Sḵwxwú7mesh, xʷməθkʷəym, səlilwəta?ł Lands. *Photo by Jamie-Leigh Ganzales.*

Christa Couture is an award-winning performing and recording artist, a non-fiction writer, and broadcaster. She is also proudly Indigenous (Cree), disabled, a mom, and queer. Her fourth album, *Long Time Leaving*, was released in 2016 on Black Hen Music; her writing has been published in *Room, Shameless, Augur*, and the anthology *The M Word*. As a speaker and storyteller, she has

addressed audiences for CBC's DNTO, Moses Znaimer's conference ideacity, and Imaginate in Port Hope, Ontario. Prairie-raised, Christa spent 17 years in Vancouver and now calls Toronto home. *Photo by Natalia Dolan.*

Corin Browne is a media producer, community engaged artist and film teacher. She co-founded the nationally recognized Summer Visions Film Institute for Youth in 1999, is the co-director of Housing Matters Media Project, Common Notions: Handbook Not Required and EMMA Talks. She is finishing a book called *We Are Everywhere: Stories of Wisdom from Former Youth in Care* and is teaching Media Arts at Templeton Secondary School. Corin parents two amazing and creative kids and collaborates often with her partner, John.

Chief Janice George / Chepximiya Siyam is a master weaver and teaching artist from the Squamish Nation. She is proud to have attended Capilano University, the Institute of American Indian Arts, and interned at the Canadian Museum of History the National Museum. Janice learned to weave from Susan Pavel and Subiyay-t Bruce Miller of Skokomish in October 2003, and is grateful

to have had many spiritual, cultural, and scholarly mentors. She began teaching in Squamish Territory and continues to travel, sharing technical, spiritual, and generational teachings. For the last fourteen years, Janice has been teaching all the way to the top of Salish-speaking Territory with her husband Buddy Joseph (Skwetsimeltxw). She is grateful to be part of this exciting time in the history of Salish People. Together with her students, she is honoured to have taught over 2,400 people.

Dorothy Woodend is the culture editor for *The Tyee*. Her work has been published in magazines, newspapers, and books across Canada and the US. Dorothy worked with the Vancouver International Film Festival, the Whistler Film Festival, and the National Film Board of Canada. She is a member of the Broadcast Film Critics Association, The Vancouver Film Critics Circle, and the Alliance of Women Film Journalists. Dorothy is also the senior festival advisor for DOXA Documentary Film Festival in Vancouver.

Helen Hughes was born and raised in BC. She started a free school for her daughter whose spirit was dying in regular school. Helen and the school grew up together during the next 45 years. She is now the grandmother of four and the matriarch of the school.

Jamie-Leigh Gonzales loves the land and the stories that come from it, and she celebrates ancestors from here and afar. She is a photographer, poet, podcast creator, and filmmaker, living on the unceded land of the Coast Salish people. Through all her creative endeavours she aims to centre community. Her poetry draws on the intersections of identity, independence, companionship and femininity. *Photo by Megan Posnikoff*

Julie Martin was born and raised in the Vancouver area, and now lives in Washington state. When not gardening or hiking and photographing the great northwest, Julie spends her time a student of the pen, words and all things literary.

Julie Flett studied fine arts at Concordia University in Montreal and Emily Carr University of Art + Design in Vancouver. She is a three-time Christie Harris Illustrated Children's Literature Prize recipient and the recipient of the 2017 Governor General's Award for Children's Literature. Julie is Cree-Métis and currently lives in Vancouver, BC, with her son.

Kian Cham is a community organizer residing on unceded Coast Salish territories. They like to organize fun events like Tiny Tiny Cozy Fest that bring people together while finding connection through arts and nature. *Photo by Ora Cogan.*

Kinnie Starr is a genre-defying artist blazing her own influential trail. Entirely self-trained, Starr moves from hip hop to art-pop, folk to spoken word to EDM with eclectic grace. Her music is fearless, intuitive, politically charged and melodic, challenging listeners while making them bounce and nod. In 2000, after leaving Mercury/Island/Def Jam, she was one of the first beatmakers to mix pow wow and hip-hop/EDM on her trilingual underground classic *Red % X* which featured Ulali. Starr produces her own music, making her one of the 5% of female producers worldwide—a growing populace she spearheads by example. She investigates the complex conversation around the gender gap in music production and authorship with her 2016 feature length documentary, *Play Your Gender*, directed by Stephanie Clattenburg in collaboration with Starr, produced by Sahar Yousefi, and co-written by all three women. www.kinniestarr.ca. *Photo by Ryan Nolan.*

Lara Messersmith-Glavin is an editor, performer, and coach based in Portland, Oregon. She is on the board of the Institute for Anarchist Studies and serves on the editorial collective of their journal, *Perspectives on Anarchist Theory*. Her own writing focuses on women, science, mythology, and commercial fishing in Alaska, where she grew up. When she's not teaching in a classroom or a gym, she can be found cursing into microphones at venues around the Pacific Northwest, going to metal shows, or exploring the woods with her child.

Leanne Betasamosake Simpson is a renowned Michi Saagiig Nishnaabeg scholar, writer and artist, who has been widely recognized as one of the most compelling Indigenous voices of her generation. Her work breaks open the intersections between politics, story and song—bringing audiences into a rich and layered world of sound, light, and sovereign creativity. Her latest book, *As We Have Always Done: Indigenous Freedom Through Radical Resistance*, was published by the University of Minnesota Press in the fall of 2017, and was awarded Best Subsequent Book by the Native American and Indigenous Studies Association. Leanne is Michi Saagiig Nishnaabeg and a member of Alderville First Nation. www.leannesimpson.ca. *Photo by Zahra Siddiqui.*

Maneo Refiloe Mohale is a South African editor, feminist writer and poet. Her work has appeared in various local and international publications, including Jalada, HOLAA!, The Beautiful Project, Prufrock Magazine, *Mail & Guardian*, and Expound Magazine. She was the 2016 Bitch Media Global Feminism Writing Fellow, where she wrote on various topics, including race, media, queerness and survivorship. She has been longlisted twice for the Sol Plaatje European Union Poetry Anthology Award for her poems, "Everything Is A Deathly Flower" and "Difaqane". In 2017, she was managing editor of Platform Media and served as Acting Arts Editor for the *Mail & Guardian* for four editions of *Mail & Guardian Friday*. She is now a Senior Media coordinator for Arts and Culture at Collective Media, an up-and-coming media and communications cooperative. www.mmohale.journoportfolio.com.

Margaret Killjoy is a transfeminine author and editor currently based in the Appalachian Mountains. Her most recent book is an anarchist demon-hunters novella, *The Barrow Will Send What It May*, published by Tor.com. She spends her time crafting and complaining about authoritarian power structures and she blogs at birdsbeforethestorm.net.

Michelle Lorna Nahanee is a member of the Squamish Nation. She grew up in Eslha7an and then East Vancouver and works within the intersection of class, race, culture and creativity. As a communications consultant and designer, Michelle has worked on social justice projects for Indigenous organizations across Canada and also within her own Nation. From health promotion to

gender equity, Michelle's collaborations have influenced opinions, changed behaviours and mobilized community action. She is a supportive leader who is most comfortable behind the scenes—contributing to social impact projects for the last 20 years. Michelle has a GED from Native Education Centre, an honours media diploma from BCIT, a Bachelor of Professional Communications from RRU and recently completed a Master of Arts in Communications at SFU with a thesis on disseminating decolonizing practices. She is the Board Chair of Kwi Awt Stelmexw and a Board Member for Pacific Association of First Nations Women. Michelle is grateful for her teachings and is always hopeful for the work ahead. *Photo by K. Ho.*

Shaunga Tagore is a writer, astrologer, performer, and a brown femme queer unicorn co-creator with the Universe. She's a proud cat mama, a Buffy enthusiast, and loves talking about death, love, and TV. www.shaungatagore.com.

Silvia Federici is a feminist activist, writer, and a teacher. In 1972 she was one of the cofounders of the International Feminist Collective, the organization that launched the Wages For Housework campaign internationally. In the 1990s, after a period of teaching and research in Nigeria, she was

active in the anti-globalization movement and the US anti–death penalty movement. She is one of the co-founders of the Committee for Academic Freedom in Africa, an organization dedicated to generating support for the struggles of students and teachers in Africa against the structural adjustment of African economies and educational systems. From 1987 to 2005 she taught international studies, women studies, and political philosophy courses at Hofstra University in Hempstead, NY. All through these years she has written books and essays on philosophy and feminist theory, women's history, education and culture, and more recently the worldwide struggle against capitalist globalization and for a feminist reconstruction of the commons.

Tasnim Nathoo is a social worker and writer who lives in Vancouver, BC (Coast Salish territories). Her work focuses on mental health and substance use, healing from trauma, and healing justice. Her writing spans topics ranging from parenting and deschooling to finding your destiny and rebellious vegetables.

Tasha Nijjar is a settler of Punjabi descent living in Vancouver on the unceded territory of the Sḵwx̱wú7mesh (Squamish), xʷməθkʷəy̓əm (Musqueam), and səlililw̓ətaʔɬ (Tsleil-Waututh) Peoples. She is passionate about exploring how creativity and social change overlap. She has worked with various community and youth-led organizations using art, film, theatre, and social media to amplify grassroots voices. She does not believe in colonial borders and has worked on campaigns around migrant justice and Indigenous solidarity. You can often find Tasha wearing big earrings, spending time with her adorable nieces and nephews, and talking trash about patriarchy with the people she loves.

Vivek Shraya is an artist whose body of work crosses the boundaries of music, literature, visual art, and film. Her album with Queer Songbook Orchestra, *PartTime Woman*, was included in CBC's list of Best Canadian Albums of 2017. Her first book of poetry, *Even This Page is White*, won a 2017 Publisher Triangle Award. Her best-selling new book, *I'm Afraid of Men*, was heralded by *Vanity Fair* as "cultural rocket fuel." She is one-half of the music duo Too Attached and the founder of the publishing imprint vs. Books.

Vivienne McMaster is a photographer, body-acceptance advocate, and creator of the Be Your Own Beloved workshops. She works with folks to help them feel empowered and resilient and to cultivate body acceptance in photographs, be it in front of their own lens or in a photo session. She has had the honour of being event photographer for the EMMA Talks series. You can read more about her at www.beyourownbeloved.com.

Walidah Imarisha is an educator, writer, public scholar and poet. She is the co-editor of two anthologies including *Octavia's Brood: Science Fiction Stories From Social Justice Movements*. Imarisha is also the author of *Angels with Dirty Faces: Three Stories of Crime, Prison and Redemption*, which won a 2017 Oregon Book Award, and the poetry collection *Scars/Stars*. She spent six years with Oregon Humanities' Conversation Project as a public scholar facilitating programs across the state about Oregon Black history, alternatives to incarceration, and the history of hip hop. She was one of the founders and first editor of political hip hop magazine *AWOL*. Imarisha taught in Stanford University's Program in Writing and Rhetoric, Pacific

Northwest College of the Arts's Critical Studies department, Portland State University's Black Studies department, and Oregon State University's Women, Gender, and Sexuality Studies department. *Photo by Pete Shaw.*